Lilith Untamed

A Guide to the Astrological Black Moon

Christina Rodenbeck

THE WESSEX ASTROLOGER

Published in 2026 by The Wessex Astrologer Ltd
PO Box 9307
Swanage
BH19 9BF
England

For a full list of our titles go to www.wessexastrologer.com

ISBN: 9781916625372

Cover design by Nell Wood
Typeset by Kevin Moore

A catalogue record for this book is available at The British Library

The Stranger

She speaks with a trace of barbarous seas,
With a voice of garbled seaweed or sand;
She offers a prayer to a god without weight or form;
She is old like one on the threshold of death.
That garden of ours which she made strange for us
Has sprung cactus and unstoppable weeds,
She draws inspiration from the desert's wind
And has loved with a whitening passion
That never finds voice, and if it did,
Would be like the map of another star.
She will live among us eighty long years,
But will always be the new arrival
Speaking a stuttering tongue of lament
Which only little animals can understand,
And she will die in our midst
On a night when she is suffering most,
With only her destiny for a pillow.
She will die the silent death of the foreigner.

Gabriela Mistral

Translated by Ciaran Cosgrove

Table of Contents

Introduction

Somewhere inside you there is a wildness that yearns to be acknowledged and seen, honoured and cherished, brought into the light. That untamed sliver of self is in all of us — and getting to know it makes us more complete and therefore more powerful, more free and more creative.

There is a perfectly practical way to explore your own inner forests and oceans, and that is using astrology.

Through my work as an astrologer, I see a lot of people on a one-to-one basis. I wouldn't call them clients really — more collaborators since we're working together to create meaning, unpick patterns and imagine a better future. People often come to me with their lives like tangled balls of wool — and we work together pulling out the colours, matching and mismatching, darning and knitting until we can see the life like a beautiful Fair Isle jumper, a singing pattern of colour and geometry. Over the years, it's become clear that one of the most essential astrological skeins, a deeply-coloured strand of wool that knits so much together, is the Black Moon Lilith.

This obscure mathematical point, unused by astrologers until the 1930s, has turned out to be the key to self-understanding for so many of the people I work with. For some of my collaborators, getting to know their own Lilith turned out to be life-changing.

In the World

But she is not just an element of your own soul pattern, she is also in the outer world. You may see her walking down the street, or glimpse her in a café, or read about her (or him because she is not always a she) in the news. Lilith is in our books and on our screens; she is in our churches and temples; she is deep in our collective imagination. For artists, Lilith is vital.

By the time you finish this book, you will recognise your own version of Lilith when you see her in the mirror, and you may even ask her to step out of the glass and into the world.

Part I

Walking into the Dark

Are you ready to dive into the snake pit, under the mountain, beneath the duvet cover?

Let's take our first steps into the world of Lilith by looking into the deep past, then into the darkest part of the night sky, and then into our own hearts.

Chapter One

Who is Lilith?

We humans are a mixture: civilised and wild, tamed and untamed, raw and refined. More and less.

The untamed part of yourself may be deeply buried beneath a sediment of inhibition, good manners or even fear — or on the other hand, your untamed self may have taken over, bringing you too deep into the darkness. Unrecognised, cast-out, your untamed self will come back with a roar and a swingeing sword. Perhaps though, you are already embodying part of that untamed self in a perfectly healthy and effective way.

If you walk consciously into the darker reaches of your own wild, embrace the seething, unsettling energy there, you plug into an infinite well of creative inspiration, fertility, growth, exuberance, libido. Your appetite for life is sharpened, and your ability to find joy and excitement are magnified.

Some of us have a lot of that wild energy, and some of us house just a few stray cats roaming on the edges of our souls. Some of us need to control and focus that unruly part of our souls, and some of us need to release it. But we all need to acknowledge it, connect with it and, yes, learn to love it.

Sometimes this place of night time, of puma and shark, tarantula and singing undergrowth, becomes exterior. We may literally move into an untamed world. We find ourselves wandering in the deep canyons of dirty streets, along the edge of a battlefield, riding a horse on the beach, singing at the top of our lungs to a raving crowd — drawn to the wild spaces of the earth, the edges of civilisation, danger, losing all inhibition. The outside matches our inner night — and sometimes that's ecstatic, and sometimes it's just really, really dark.

For each of us, this untamed you is different and personal, of course, but it is also a familiar cultural figure in the collective. This may be Pan or Kali — a creature or person to be feared and revered — or it may be an outcast: witch, cunning man, prostitute, vagabond, banshee, Heathcliff, whistleblower.

This wild, instinctual energy has usually been characterised as female — but through this book, you'll see how overly rigid gendering is just another rule that needs to be broken.

For the purposes of this book, I'll be using the label of Lilith, because her story encapsulates this raw, free energy, and her name has become synonymous with rebellion, freedom and embracing the so-called dark.

She-Devil

Lilith is a Hebrew she-devil, Adam's first wife, who lives in the desert, sometime partner to the demon Samael, mother of millions, murderer of infants and mothers in labour, tickler of babies' feet, negotiator with angels, and all-round Kabbalistic bad girl, with a special home at the bottom of the Tree of Death. In short, she's a bit of a nightmare.

Today Lilith — seductress, demoness, vampire, child-killer, independent woman — is everywhere; in video games and comic books, novels and TV series, academic journals and feminist tracts, and in Texas, if you need an abortion, you might apply to the Lilith Fund. She is also in the sky above — the furthest point of the Moon's orbit from Earth is known by astrologers as Black Moon Lilith.

An archetype

Lilith is also an archetype, a concept developed by psycho-analyst Carl Jung to describe characters or ideas that seem to be part of what he termed the "collective unconscious", the giant dream we are all dreaming that is filled with universal images and myths — the wise woman, mother, father, baby, the trial, the journey, the gift, the trickster, the fool, the princess, initiation. These are all stories or types that could be recognised anywhere in the world. He explained in his essay *Wotan*, written in 1936: "An archetype is like an old watercourse along which the water of life has flowed for centuries, digging a deep channel for itself. The longer it has flowed in this channel the more likely it is that sooner or later the water will return to its old bed."

Jung's theory is that we each hold many of these archetypes within ourselves, and that we may also see them, or project them, into the outer world. They appear in myths and fairytales, and also in other forms of fiction. Jung was probably not imagining the 21st century's addiction to Marvel and DC franchises, so clearly driven by archetypal characters — Superman, X-Men, Wonder Woman — but their creators most certainly reference Jung. Yet archetypes also show up in our realities. Your wedding may have been a real life enactment of an archetype. Or perhaps that wedding was your own work of creative writing? That boss could be an archetypal Mother figure, or your neighbour a Fool. Sometimes others move in and out of archetype — is your own son sometimes the Wise Child and occasionally a Vampire?

Like all genuine archetypes, Lilith is eternal. A citizen of Sumer, a rabbi from medieval Persia, or a story-teller from 18th century Krakow would probably recognise our 21st-century description of this most famous demoness. She hasn't changed much in 4000 years.

Lilith is an archetype of the untamed, and she is flowing fast right now, growing stronger.

Origin Story

The original story of Lilith is a short and simple one. The first written example we have is in a satirical text called *The Alphabet of Ben Sira*, written sometime between 700 AD and 1000 AD in the Islamic world. Scholars suspect it was meant to be funny.

> After God created Adam, He said, "It is not good for the man to be alone. I will make a helper suitable for him."(Gen. 2:18).
>
> So God crafted a companion for the first man, a woman, shaped from the earth, just like Adam. He called her Lilith.
>
> But Adam and Lilith could not agree about the most basic part of their union. They fought about who would lie on top during intercourse. Lilith refused to lie below and Adam felt that he was superior so he should be on top.
>
> Lilith said: 'We are both created from the earth, so we are equal.'
>
> But Adam would not listen to this argument, and when Lilith understood that they would never agree, she pronounced the Ineffable Name, grew leathery wings and flew away into the air.

Adam went to God. 'Master of the universe!' he said. 'The woman you gave me has flown away.' So God sent three angels — Sanoy, Sansenoy, and Samangelof — to retrieve her.

God said to Adam, 'If she agrees to return to you, she will not be punished. But if not, she must allow one hundred of her children to die every day.'

The angels overtook Lilith in the raging waters of the Red Sea. They told her the news, but she did not wish to return to Adam.

The angels said, 'We will drown you in the sea.'

But Lilith was having none of this. 'Leave me alone!' she said. 'I was made to cause sickness to infants. Male babies will be in my power for eight days after birth, and females for 20 days.'

The angels were horrified and begged her to go back to Adam. But she swore to them by the name of the living and eternal God: "Ok, so here's a deal. If I see your names on an amulet, or even your shapes, I'll have no power over the babies."

Lilith also agreed to allow one hundred of her children die every day.

That is why every day a hundred demons perish, and for the same reason, we write the angels' names on the amulets of newborns. When Lilith sees their names, she remembers her oath, and the child will be protected from her.[1]

In other parts of Hebrew apocrypha, Lilith is said to be married to the demon Samael. She is accused of tickling babies while they are asleep, and of draining semen from men at night. She is said to be a night demon, a seductress. Sometimes she is winged. Her origins, of course, go back much further than this piece of writing. There is evidence of belief in her presence in various parts of the Mediterranean and Middle East since ancient times. But the stories are consistent and they have the following themes.

1 Based on Jewish Women's Archive. "Alphabet of Ben Sira 78: Lilith." (Viewed on November 10, 2025) <https://jwa.org/node/23210>.

The Dark Feminine

For men, Jung associated the 'Dark Feminine' with the anima or the female part of the soul. His advice: "You, man, should not seek the feminine in women, but seek and recognise it in yourself, as you possess it from the beginning." He also associated this anima energy with the yogic concept of *kundalini*, a feminine energy that snakes up the body, and believed it was crucial to personal development. "The *kundalini* in psychological terms is that which makes you go on the greatest adventure."

However, Jung's concept of the Dark Feminine plays differently for people who are not like him. He was writing from his own time and place — 20th century Switzerland, as the patriarch of a wealthy household — so his Dark Feminine was specifically his. Jung's may be the starting point for thinking of the Lilith archetype, but his ideas are not the end point.

Each archetype is many faceted — good, bad and somewhere in between. The hero becomes a tyrant, the warrior turns into a murderess, the wise child is just a fool. Understanding these characters in the round brings them into three dimensions and makes them spring to life in the stories we tell each other.

Astrological Archetypes

The fact that Jung was a practising astrologer is often suppressed by strict Jungians (and by Jung himself, who liked to keep this on the down low), but it is the case. And you can see that his descriptions of many archetypes tally with the astrological meanings of the planets. For example, Saturn is the Wise Old Man, the Mother is the Moon, the Sun is the Hero. The basis of astrology is that the energies of all the planets are contained within each of us. These different energies mix together in a kaleidoscope of colours, each filtered through the signs of the zodiac.

It's useful also to remind yourself that astrology is an ancient art with roots deep in the past, that has grown and flourished through patriarchal times, taking on specific concepts that are completely informed by that point of view. Like society itself, astrology has rejected and repressed certain archetypes. As a consequence, the Untamed has also been rejected from traditional astrology.

The Lilith archetype is just as complex as all the others, but most of the time we are shown just one side of her. She is often the symbol of specific male anxieties: castration, devouring mothers, multiplicity, rebellious women, sirens and whores, but there is much more to Lilith than that. Nor is she simply the opposite: independent, unshackled, free thinking, forthright, whole. In fact, many aspects of the Lilith archetype are traditional female fears: sexual abuse, betrayal, death in childbirth, loss of children, miscarriage, adultery.

As an archetype, versions of Lilith appear across cultures. Here are some examples.

The Hindu goddess Kali

There are several Hindu goddesses who are avatars of Lilith, but Kali is probably the most well-known. She is usually depicted as midnight black or indigo and often with her long, red tongue protruding. She wears a belt of severed heads and carries an array of weapons. Beneath her feet, you can sometimes see Shiva, the Lord of Transformation, asleep.

Her origin stories vary, but all agree that she is a personification of rage, or fury in battle, a killer of demons. In some places she is worshipped as the Supreme Mother. She is also an example of how rage, focused, has its uses.

Baba Yaga, the Slavic witch in the wild

Every Eastern European child knows of Baba Yaga, the terrifying witch who lives in a hut that stands on three chicken legs deep in the forest; who rides the skies in a mortar wielding a huge pestle. She appears in many fairy tales — testing heroes and heroines to see the limits of their fortitude, and sometimes helping out with a gift if they have performed their tasks well. Baba Yaga is both terrifying — snacking on human soup — and generous. Seeing Baba Yaga, facing the shadow, is usually an initiation for the young protagonist of a tale.

Cihuacoatl, the Aztec goddess

Cihuacoatl was usually depicted as a skull-faced woman, even though she was the goddess of midwives and childbirth. She often carries snakes, which are creatures so often associated with this archetype.

Shahmaran, a mythical creature from Anatolia

The story of Shahmaran is a Turkish folktale with very ancient roots. Shahmaran has the face of a beautiful woman, but her tail is the head of a snake. She lives deep in caves under the mountains. In the best-known tale, she falls in love with a lovely human, and teaches him all about herbs and medicines. One day he decides to return to the surface. After many years and many mishaps, Shahmaran is murdered in a bath, but her lover manages to drink the water of the bath — thus imbibing all of her wisdom and becoming a doctor.

O winged Lady,
Like a bird
You scavenge the land.
Like a charging storm
You charge,
Like a roaring storm
You roar,
You thunder in thunder,
Snort in rampaging winds.
Your feet are continually restless.
Carrying your harp of sighs,
You breathe out the music of mourning.

— **extract from 'Hymn to Inanna'**
by Enheduanna,
translated from the Sumerian by Jane Hirshfield

European Shapeshifters

In France, there are tales of a magical water sprite, named Melusine, whose lower half turned into a snake sometimes. There are many versions of her story. In one tale, she marries the Count of Poitou, bears him 10 children and then turns into a dragon and flies off.

In Northern countries, there are many tales of the selkie, a woman who was sometimes a seal. You could only catch her and keep her if you could hide the sealskin she shed sometimes. Selkies were said to be tremendously alluring, but essentially wild.

The Sumerian sea-monster Tiamet

Known as the glistening one, she was the mother of gods and monsters, creatrix, goddess of primordial chaos. Like her European counterparts, she was sometimes a woman and sometimes a mythical sea creature.

Lamia, Medusa, Artemis, Pan

There are echoes of this wild, untamed energy across classical literature. Lilith was Lamia, devourer of children, or Medusa of the snake-hair, or Artemis, goddess of the wild and of the crescent Moon. Artemis was the twin of Apollo, a god of light and civilisation, his opposite and equal, known for her freedom, the wild girls who followed her in the woods, and

Here are some examples of how Lilith appears as an archetype.

1. Rebel woman — independent woman
2. Wild woman — innocent in the wilderness
3. Adulteress, seductress, sexual vampire — erotic, sexually liberated
4. Abuse victim — avenger
5. Killer of infants — mother of millions
6. Independent woman — serial killer
7. Femme fatale — sexually satisfied
8. Joker
9. Extraordinary or prolific talent

her prowess as a hunter. Many tried, but no man or god could ever possess her — and those who tried came to sticky ends.

Lilith also bears a resemblance to the Greek god Pan, the god of the wild, who like Artemis, eschewed the towns and cities, preferring instead to play his pipes in the mountains. Unlike Artemis, though, Pan was a randy god, copulating with humans, immortals and animals with abandon. If you woke Pan from his afternoon nap, curled up under an ancient oak, perhaps, on the side of some Arcadian hill, his shout might send you into a panic, driving you briefly mad. We will see that the astrological Lilith can appear as sexually voracious or virginal, or both at once, and she too can drive you insane.

There are other male gods with whom Lilith has an affinity, for example, the ancient Egyptian god, Seth, lord of chaos and the desert. Like Seth, she represents things the 'civilised' world fears, is disgusted by, or rejects.

Othering

Negative descriptions of Lilith constantly describe the cultural 'other' — savage, rebellious, uncivilised, barbaric, sexually promiscuous, uncontrolled. Specifically, racist accounts of other people are often descriptions of Adam's first wife. For example: Jews accused of murdering babies in the Middle Ages, Africans described as savages, loose white women in Bollywood movies, nearly everything written about enslaved Americans for about 400 years. Descriptions of witches during the European witch hunts are word-for-word descriptions of Lilith: lovers of Satan, child killers, seducers.

As an archetype of the untamed, of wildness, liberation, taboo-busting, boundary burning, naked dancing and more, untamed Lilith or a version of her is there inside you. But I want to be clear about your untamed self: it's gender-fluid. Lilith is a convenient handle. For some of us, the Dark Feminine that she represents will be just that, for others it's a feeling that's more akin to Dionysus, the Greek god of insanity and wildness. This energy is liberating, so you should feel free when you get in touch with it, not constricted by anyone's iron definitions of what is or is not true Lilith or true wild. Does nature itself really have a gender? I leave that up to you to ponder.

Finding Lilith

When Lilith is suppressed, ignored or put down, she gets angry and sad and dangerous. She may burst out violently, or wither away, taking your creativity and curiosity with her. Often, but not always, she is the rejected part of you, the non-conformist squeezed into a business suit, the tomboy, the boy in a tutu, the hermit on the edge of town, the whore, the tramp, the savage. She may be someone you knew well when you were a child, but have spent years containing. Or she may have overwhelmed your life, dragging you down and out, into the gutter and into rage, or to the very pinnacle of your profession. She is in all of us somewhere, bursting to get out and show herself, and pull us to the edge of life, the end of love — and sometimes over the precipice into real peril or violence.

Key adjectives for Lilith energy: wild, untamed, creative, erotic, unboundaried, uncivilised, on the edge, funny, dangerous, violent, crazy, unstable, outcast, disgusting, scary, vulgar, violent, vengeful, sexy, alluring, non-conformist, unconventional, outlandish, alive, natural, hysterical, talented, repulsive.

Lilith in Art

If you have ever seen a real flamenco dancer, or listened to a soul singer like British artist Amy Winehouse or the Lebanese diva Fairuz or beautiful Marvin Gaye, then you may have felt *duende*.

This is a Spanish word used to explain that exhilarating sensation which both the performer and the audience feel when in the presence of something otherworldly arriving in the performance. A critic of flamenco or singing in Spain might say when the performer is channeling Lilith: "This has *duende*." The Spanish poet Federico Garcia Lorca explained *duende*, in a famous lecture given in 1933, as "dark sounds", "the roots that cling to the mire that we all know, that we all ignore, but from which comes the very substance of art," a "mysterious force that everyone feels and no philosopher has explained."

It's something that blues singers recognise as 'soul'. But Lorca went further than that. He said that all art from dance to sculpture could have *duende*. "So, then, the *duende* is a force not a labour, a struggle not a thought…Seeking the *duende*, there is neither map nor discipline. We only know it burns the blood like powdered glass, that it exhausts, rejects all the sweet geometry we understand, that it shatters styles and makes Goya, master of the greys, silvers and pinks... paint with his knees and fists in terrible bitumen blacks."

So *duende* — melancholy, wild, earthy, authentic

Use your imagination — or someone else's

If there is one fictional character that you feel might express your inner Lilith — wild, free, untamed, unlikely — which existing character would that be?

Remember this is not a fixed thing, but just think of it now, quickly. Don't overthink. Don't fix it to any previous construct you have of, say, the 'Dark Feminine'. It might help if you think of someone of the opposite sex?

For me, just for today, it's the 'Man with No Name' in *The Good, the Bad and the Ugly*, poncho, cigar and boots. Clint Eastwood is my Lilith.

I asked my friend, a gentle, male psychotherapist, who he would choose. He replied instantly, "Angelina Jolie as *Maleficent*. Not a great movie, but a superb hat."

So have fun with this. It's often someone unexpected, jarring, funny that you encounter.

permeates and elevates all art forms. Lorca contrasts *duende* to a muse or a guardian angel; both of these, he says, come from outside, but "the duende surges up, inside, from the soles of the feet." Without true duende, an artist is just doing the motions. The force called *duende* is Lilith rising.

There is another important aspect of Lilith for artists, and for all of us. Lilith unleashed can be an unstoppable urge to ignore restrictions, to break boundaries. Lilith refuses to be contained in the old ways. Real creativity goes beyond skill and talent, deeper and further connecting the tamed and untamed self, and even the tamed and untamed collective.

Hollywood's Warring Liliths

During Hollywood's Golden Age, at the same time Lilith was first being put to use in astrology in the 1930s, the two greatest female stars in Tinsel Town were dramatising two opposite faces of Lilith.

Joan Crawford and Bette Davis, powerhouse actresses with screen personae that melted the celluloid, loathed each other. Their lifelong rivalry incubated in the 1930s, and perhaps culminated in that camp cult classic *Whatever Happened to Baby Jane?* (1962), which capitalised on their infamous rivalry.

Both embody styles of Lilith — and, of course, it turns out, their Liliths are in opposing signs. Lilith can show us where we have a well of inspiration, and both drew on their real-life backgrounds to create their film roles.

Davis has Lilith in the sign of royalty, nobility, entitlement, and acting, Leo, while Crawford's is in the sign of Aquarius — popularity, the common person, equality.

This is precisely reflected in the kinds of parts they played, and in their personal backgrounds. Crawford had dragged herself up from a poverty-stricken childhood in Texas, whereas Davis was a privileged East Coast Brahmin. Davis played posh people and Crawford played women who had made it to the top through grit. Both were declared 'box office poison' in the late 1930s, but came back stronger in the 1940s.

Two roles stand out. Davis in *All About Eve* plays a famous stage actress, whose stardom is usurped by a younger rival. In the film, Davis, like the Biblical Lilith, is replaced by another woman. This theme of rivalry is one which we'll explore later in the book.

Crawford was the mistress of expressing raw, untamed passion beneath a still mask. It's all in the eyes. Perhaps the role that expresses this most forcefully, is the obsessive, guilt-ridden Louise, in *Possessed* (1947), which nearly won Crawford an Oscar. In it she plays a nurse to a wealthy family, who is driven mad by her own sense of guilt, and a passionate obsession with a younger man. It's a thrilling performance because of the focused way Crawford releases her wild self.

Knowing Your Lilith

Instead of being frightened or overwhelmed, you can choose to get to know your own Lilith. You can embrace that patch of inner night, consciously, creatively — and lovingly. Even stray cats thrive in a home. You could do this by deliberate meditation, if that's your expertise, through a shamanic journey, or through psycho-analytic work. You have certainly met her in your dreams.

Lilith's power, her exuberance, her lust for living to the very edges of your life is available to you. Acknowledge your own Lilith, embrace her (or him or them, for each of us Lilith is universal and unique), and transform your life into something fuller, richer, deeper, more fulfilling.

You can also reject her, suppress her, contain her, ignore her: but one day she will sweep you into her obscure embrace. Sometimes the night where she takes you will be very dark indeed, a starless waste where monsters roam, a basement, a prison, a terror, cruelty, madness. Sometimes the night Lilith offers, even if you have ignored her for decades, will be the place on the edge of time and space, a place of infinity and imagination, velvet and mysterious.

Better by far to light your flaming torch, and walk willingly into the dark.

The Themes of Lilith

These tropes belong to Lilith. They may be more or less strong in your life depending on how she is activated in your chart both by transit and natal aspects.

Negative	*Positive*
1. Sexual abuse	1. Prodigious creativity
2. Miscarriage and abortion	2. Love of wilderness
3. Incest	3. Affinity with animals
4. Adultery	4. Three-way friendships
5. Enslavement	5. Magic
6. Miscarriage	6. Hilarity
7. Insanity	7. Freedom and Rebellion
8. Rage	8. Non-conforming
9. Exile	9. Joyful lust
10. Getting burnt at the stake	10. Sexual allure
11. Corruption, pollution	11. Fertility and Childbirth
	12. Thresholds

Chapter Two

The Astrological Lilith

There is one esoteric tool that directly identifies your own personal Lilith — and that is astrology. Lilith only entered the astrological lexicon in the mid-20th century, and for the most part she was ignored. However, her astrological potency is uncanny, as I will show you in this book.

By finding your astrological Lilith and understanding the meaning and significance of her placement, you will gain unmatchable insight into your own personal wildness.

It's a cosmic point I've been working with for more than a decade, testing it against the reality of my own life and the lives of friends and collaborators. Not every astrologer works in the same way, but I am one of those who wants an astrological reading to be a conversation. I like to

A Proliferation of Liliths

There are three astrological Liliths, and this blurring of definitions or confusion is part of her story too. The first two are not the subject of this book, and not significant astrologically.

1. The tiny asteroid Lilith — number 1181 — was named after her in 1927.
2. Waltemath's Lilith — this second Moon was hypothesised by German astronomer Georg Waltemath at the end of the 19th century. At the time, some, such as the English astrologer styled Sepharial, played around with this idea and named this point Lilith. There is no second Moon, but you don't need me to tell you that. Still, even astrologers confuse early 20th century references to this Lilith with those referring to the Black Moon, which do not seem to appear until the 1930s.
3. Black Moon Lilith — the one we're talking about, and the one you will find in many ephemerides.

draw out my clients' stories and see how they have lived out the potential of their natal charts and how the movement of the planets has affected them through their lives. I am a collector of stories, because I am fascinated by people, and also because hearing stories and discussing them helps us to understand the next story more profoundly. One story informs another, and then another, in a jewelled multi-dimensional web.

I became fascinated with the Black Moon Lilith as it became clear that she was often activated during specific life events — radicalisation, activism, adultery, miscarriage, exile, adoption, creative flow. It also became clear that if you were born with a powerfully active Lilith, this could be incredibly helpful rather than destructive. Some of my most successful clients were actually working unconsciously with the creative power of Lilith: as midwives, artists, firefighters, vets, feminists.

What Exactly Is The Astrological Lilith?

The 'Black Moon' Lilith that most astrologers use is not a planet or an asteroid or a star. It's a mathematical point first noted by the 17th century astronomer (and astrologer) Johannes Kepler, when he understood that the orbit of the Moon was not circular, but elliptical. However, this point was not labelled Lilith until much later.

The Lilith favoured by astrologers is the apogee of the Moon;[2] the point on the Moon's orbit that is furthest from the Earth at any given moment. The perigee is the closest point.

Despite Kepler, Black Moon Lilith is a recent addition to the astrologer's craft. The Black Moon Lilith, often referred to as BML, only came into use in the 1930s. Most astrological work on Lilith has been done in France,[3] Germany and the Netherlands.

Some western astrologers have dismissed Lilith as just an invisible mathematical point and therefore unlikely to have any effect. However, there is a powerful precedent for using invisible points. The North and South Nodes of the Moon, which are also notional points in the sky,

---

2 There is one school of thought that Black Moon Lilith is the void point within the orbit of the Moon around the Earth. Astrologically, this is sort of nitpicking, since both points will be on the same degree of the zodiac. But it is worth noting that there is endless confusion about exactly where the astrological Lilith lies.

3 In particular the work of French astrologer Luc Bigé is worth reading.

have been used since ancient times, and within Vedic astrology they are critically important, given as much weight as the planets. Named *rahu* and *ketu*, the North and South Node take their place next to the more commonly known planets outside temples in India. In the West they are known as the Dragon's Head and the Dragon's Tail, and many astrologers understand that they are extremely potent.

Astrologers occasionally discuss the significance of the time that energies enter the collective consciousness via the discovery of planets or other phenomena. For example Uranus the 'rebel' was discovered in 1781 at a time of revolution in the USA and France; and Pluto, discovered in 1931, heralded the atomic age. Some astrologers argue that the arrival of new planets brings forth energies that have always been there, but that are now ready to be acknowledged.

So it's quite noteworthy that the two most clearly 'problematic' astrological forces[4] — Pluto and Lilith — came into play in the lead up to World War II. Importantly, Lilith's arrival in the 1930s also coincided with increasing liberation for women around the globe, and greater political, economic and social power. In short, the fifty per cent of humanity that had been, for centuries or even millennia, suppressed and oppressed, began to gain power. As we'll see, there is correlation between Lilith and the astrology of feminists, women's liberation, and, in contrast, misogyny and sexual abuse: astrology works along axes and with opposites.

What follows in this book is from my own observations, after working with Lilith in hundreds of charts. Since Lilith is a new element to work with and relatively unresearched (at least in the Anglosphere), I have started from scratch and tested whether assumptions about Lilith actually hold water. So over the years I have paid attention when natal Liliths have received significant transits, or when transiting Lilith has made a significant aspect to someone's natal chart. I've also simply noted the powerful natal Liliths in some charts, and discussed with clients how this manifests through their life experience.

4 Another candidate for most troublesome planet is Eris, the goddess of chaos, whose meddling malice caused the Trojan War. She was discovered in 2005.

The Lilith in You

In astrology, you cannot tell the difference between a man's chart and a woman's chart. They look the same. You may be a man or a woman or non-binary, you still contain the spirit of Lilith, of Jupiter, of Venus.

On the day you were born, the Black Moon Lilith was at a particular point in the sky, which astrologers mark as one of the 360 degrees of the zodiac. Each sign — from Aries to Pisces — takes up 30° of that circle. So your Lilith might be at say, 15° Pisces or 2° Aries. This sign placement will tell you the style of Lilith you have; what your untamed self might feel like. You will share this Lilith sign with a cohort of people born within nine months.

Black Moon Lilith takes just under nine years to go around the entire zodiac, and spends nine months in a sign, and nine days in a degree. This means that many people born in the same year are likely to have been born with Lilith in the same sign. It's an interesting exercise to look at your classmates for aspects of that particular Lilith and see how they are different from those born a little earlier or later with a different Lilith sign.

This makes Lilith a somewhat generational point by sign. Indeed, she is the first such generational indicator, as her orbit is shorter than Jupiter's (12 months), but longer than the asteroids (usually around four months). You are likely to share Jupiter, Saturn, Uranus, Neptune and Pluto placements with a much wider cohort.

Astrology will show you how to locate your own Lilith, your untamed self. This is the basis for learning to focus that powerful energy more consciously.

The Via Lamia

The apogee of the Moon wobbles as it moves through the sky, so there is a 'true' or oscillating Lilith which moves forward and backwards erratically, and an average or 'mean' Lilith which ticks forward like a clock. Normally, it is the mean Lilith that is used in astrology, but both are valuable. In this book, the mean Lilith is used unless otherwise stated. Again, another blurring of Lilith.

The space between the true and mean Lilith can create a kind of power corridor in the chart, which I label the *Via Lamia*.[5] This can be as wide as 28 degrees, or both the mean and true may be on the same point.

If the *Via Lamia* is very wide, it's more likely that you'll have a variety of ways that Lilith is expressed. The Via can cut across houses and signs, so it's worth looking at all of these. On the other hand, a tightly focused Via of 1-5 degrees suggests great intensity around the things of Lilith and by no means weakens her power.

Throughout this book, you will find examples of how Lilith has manifested in the lives of others — from Marilyn Monroe to my mother — and I'll explain how Lilith works astrologically for these people too. But although these stories are pinned down by astrological analysis, this book is aimed at helping everyone, including people with no knowledge of astrology at all.

Let these real-life stories guide and inspire. Throughout this book I also recommend books, poems, songs, paintings, movies and TV shows that can help you feel and explore Lilith more powerfully. Together, they should create a visual and emotional pathway to deeper understanding for your own untamed self.

5 The Dutch astrologer Dick Van Der Mark has done some interesting work on this.

Part II

Embodying Lilith

If Lilith is an archetype, then we can find her and her story in our own world — through history, politics, personal stories, literature, myth, movies.

In the following chapters I will use astrology to help you locate the untamed part of yourself. We'll look at the operation of the Black Moon Lilith through the signs and houses. If you want to skip to your own sign and house placement, please do so, but I suggest you also read the others as this will give you a greater feel for this energy, which will ebb and flow and evolve through your lifetime.

Chapter Three

The Signs of the Zodiac

The signs of the zodiac from Aries to Pisces are like 12 different flavours through which passes the essence of each cosmic symbol — from the mighty Sun to Lilith herself.

The sign shows us how Lilith might express herself in your character. Will she be mint-flavoured like Virgo? Or will she come through smelling of peach blossom and champagne?

Under each heading I have included quotations from people who have Lilith in that particular sign, and I've also included a self-portrait by an artist with that Lilith placement. Note these well, because they should start to come together to form a mosaic of how Lilith is working in that sign. Remember her effects, like those of all the cosmic gods and goddesses, are varied and will differ from person to person, but they do fall into the themes listed in the previous chapter.

Self-portrait. Henri Matisse. Lilith in Aries.

Aries

"If you're lonely when you're alone, you're in bad company."

— Jean-Paul Sartre

"I want to keep smashing myself until I am whole."

— Elias Canetti, *The Human Province*

"The principal mark of genius is not perfection but originality, the opening of new frontiers."

— Arthur Koestler

"There is no intensity of love or feeling that does not involve the risk of crippling hurt. It is a duty to take this risk, to love and feel without defence or reserve."

— William S. Burroughs

Lilith in Aries

21 January 1905 –17 October 1905
26 November 1913–23 August 1914
1 October 1922–29 June 1923
6 August 1931–3 May 1932
11 June 1940–8 March 1941
16 April 1949–12 January 1950
19 February 1958–17 November 1958
26 December 1966–22 September 1967
31 October 1975–27 July 1976
5 September 1984–1 June 1985
11 July 1993–7 April 1994
17 May 2002–10 February 2003
23 March 2011–3 December 2011
27 January 2020–21 October 2020
2 December 2028–26 August 2029

"No one behind, no one ahead.
The path the ancients cleared has closed.
And the other path, everyone's path,
easy and wide, goes nowhere.
I am alone and find my way."

— Adapted from Sanskrit by Octavio Paz

"That she had so completely recovered her sanity was a source of sadness to her. One should never be cured of one's passion."

— Marguerite Duras, *The Ravishing of Lol Stein*

Maybe my passion is nothing special, but at least it's mine."

— Tove Jansson, *Travelling Light*

> "You know the name you were given, you do not know the name that you have."
>
> — José Saramago, *All the Names*

> "If anything happiness is a feeling of being essential."
>
> — Fay Weldon

> "To exist is to drink oneself without thirst."
>
> — Annie Ernaux, *Les Années*

The sign of the Ram, the first of the zodiac: initiator, absolute beginner, warrior. Passionate, brave, focused, innocent, fiery. Aries is the sign of the beginning, hatching, opening. It's the start; the initiation. And the Black Moon Lilith in this part of the zodiac brings significant wild energy to these themes.

This means that you may be brilliant at starting things off, setting out on adventures. You may also have a highly competitive streak. Some may have a need to come first that's so strong they are willing to cheat, a passion for starting things that's overwhelming.

Lilith's love of wilderness and nature can be more pronounced in Aries. Wilderness as a place of refuge or a place of retreat. I have a client who fairly regularly goes on wild pilgrimages — mushing in Alaska, the midnight sun in Lapland, diving in fjords. She is also a person who participates in initiations as an assistant in shamanic ceremonies. This is interesting because Lilith is in her seventh house of partnership.

Aries is often a physical sign. And several clients are unusually physically brave, and frankly foolhardy with this placement, unable to see their own limitations until they have an accident. But that same physicality can be magically enhanced with Lilith in Aries. One client has Lilith two degrees from her Midheaven, the highest point, and marker of career and status. She is a bodyworker specialising in pregnant women and childbirth. She is a remarkably tall and striking woman, who looks like a heroine from a Norse saga, able to hurl boulders, birth children and keep tribal peace. In other times, she would literally have been a physical beacon.

Pina Bausch, the surreal and marvellous German choreographer, started her career as a solo performer. Here is the citation for her European Theatre Award, VII Edition.

> "Since she took over the direction of the Wuppertal Tanztheater 25 years ago, Pina Bausch has used her training and experience as a soloist in classical ballet to literally invent a new genre, a combination of theatre, dance, music, and visual arts in which score and improvisation come together, very close to the dream of a total theatre that juxtaposes the individual talents of an extraordinary ensemble with a precise concept of time and space..."

That pretty much sums up some of the ground-breaking potential of Lilith in Aries. Bausch's is in her ninth house of shared knowledge and makes a perfect trine to her Sun-Pluto conjunction in Leo, the sign of performance in her twelfth house of collective dreaming. She said: "It is almost unimportant whether a work finds an understanding audience. One has to do it because one believes that it is the right thing to do. We are not only here to please, we cannot help challenging the spectator."

Lilith really doesn't care what other people think.

Another example of Lilith in Aries pioneering mode is Christian Barnard, the first person to perform a heart transplant. On the day of the surgery, 3 December 1967, Saturn, the planet of mastery and steadiness, conjoined his daring Lilith.

Hitler's architect, Albert Speer, is also an interesting example of Lilith in Aries. His Lilith makes a conjunction to Mercury, the planet of communications in the ninth house of publishing. Speer was tried at Nuremberg and spent twenty years in jail, where he passed his time reading and creating an elaborate garden. When he was released he spent his remaining years creating the 'Speer myth' of the 'good Nazi'. This has since been shown to be a fabrication, but it's interesting to see the darker side of Lilith here, working with Mercury, the planet of storytelling and communications. Lilith energy is not about the truth, and this is an important way in which she differs from her colleague Pluto.

Lilith was in Aries during the first year of the COVID-19 pandemic. Clearly, other astrological factors were involved with COVID, the lockdown, the economic fallout and the swirl of lies and conspiracy theories that year. However, there was one aspect of the lockdown, especially the first one in the early part of 2020, that had a feel of Lilith in Aries — a return to square one in nature. There were pictures of deer on highways, foxes walking down the middle of the street, wild boar wandering through backyards.

Sharon Stone

Movie star Sharon Stone is a Pisces Sun with Lilith in Aries, in an out-of-sign conjunction, and her story is a classic Lilith tale.

Her breakout role was in a film-noir-ish tale which came out in 1990, called *Basic Instinct*. In the movie, Stone plays a bisexual serial killer — letting her Lilith out, and expressing archetypal male fears. This is a pre-#MeToo Hollywood. There's also a famous shot when the camera looks right at Stone's vulva. Vaginas are Lilith's territory — with or without teeth. So are shame and shamelessness.

Stone has since said that she was tricked into doing the shot. Now, here's the interesting part. She has the Lilith experience, which is deeply shaming, but years later Stone has used that moment to reclaim her shame. In fact, she's done that not by denying or hiding, but by taking things further and using her fame to discuss sexual abuse. So her innocent Lilith in warrior Aries, wounded in childhood, abused in young adulthood comes back as a warrior in later life.

Wildflowers were rampant that spring. For a brief moment it was easy to imagine the world rewilding. If we stopped for a moment, maybe Lilith could start at the beginning again growing her wild garden.

That is probably rather fanciful, but collectively when Lilith transits through Aries every nine years we can expect some kind of beginning again, however mild or temporary, of a Lilith theme.

Some famous people with Lilith in Aries

Norman Mailer, John Updike, Imre Nagy, Josef Stalin, John Lennon, Pamela Anderson, Albert Einstein, Justin Bieber, Katy Perry, Scarlett Johanssen, Michael Jackson, Prince Harry, Mahatma Gandhi

Best: groundbreaking

Worst: self-harming

Taurus

"We are all born mad. Some remain so."

— Samuel Beckett

"This terrifying world is not devoid of charms, of the mornings that make waking up worthwhile."

— Wislawa Szymborska

"The inferno of the living is not something that will be; if there is one, it is what is already here, the inferno where we live every day, that we form by being together. There are two ways to escape suffering it. The first is easy for many: accept the inferno and become such a part of it that you can no longer see it. The second is risky and demands constant vigilance and apprehension: seek and learn to recognise who and what, in the midst of inferno, are not inferno, then make them endure, give them space."

— Italo Calvino

"I like this word decadent; all shimmering and purple and gold."

— Paul Verlaine

"Here are fruits, flowers, leaves and branches, and here is my heart which beats only for you."

— Paul Verlaine

"I shut my eyes and all the world drops dead;
I lift my lids and all is born again"

— Sylvia Plath, 'Mad Girl's Love Song'

"What would the world be, once bereft
Of wet and of wildness? Let them be left,
O let them be left, wildness and wet;
Long live the weeds and the wilderness yet."

— Gerard Manley Hopkins, 'Inversnaid'

"To be great, be whole;
Exclude nothing, exaggerate nothing that is not you.
Be whole in everything. Put all you are

Self-Portrait. Dora Wahlroos. Lilith in Taurus

Into the smallest thing you do.
Who is this?
So, in each lake, the moon shines with splendour
Because it blooms up above."

— Fernando Pessoa, 'Odes'

"If we are to achieve things never before accomplished we must employ methods never before attempted"

— Francis Bacon

Once upon a time, at the beginning of time, there was a beautiful garden. Hibiscus and melons, pomegranates and strawberries, lions and lemurs: all nature thrived there. And at the centre of that lush, fruitful garden were two humans, but one refused to be dominated by the other, and she was cast out.

Fixed earthy Taurus is the sign of nature in abundance, gardens in spring, blossoming, fecundity, sensuality, fertility, indeed it is the sign of Eden. Ruled by Venus, the goddess of love and beauty, art and charm, Taurus is the sign associated with all five senses. Taurus creates harmony and order, balance and beauty.

And here is Lilith in that Eden — Adam's first wife. She's at home — at least for a while — with her feet rooting in the soil, her hair twining

Lilith Returns: Artistic Outpouring

In February 1888, the Dutch artist Vincent Van Gogh moved to Arles, a city in southern France, a place where his work suddenly exploded with vibrancy and colour, and he found himself swept up into a creative maelstrom. That year, Van Gogh was also experiencing his Lilith Return. The transit which happens every nine years when Lilith comes back to the same position where she was when you are born.

The fact that Van Gogh was a pioneer is probably to do with his Aries Sun. His unique vision is channelled through his planets in Pisces, but the sensuality of his painting comes across as Lilith in Taurus, visceral, unstoppable. His feel for the texture of paint is unique. And in his life, he acted out that Lilith, an outcast from society, painting on the edge of town, rejected by his fellow artists, thrown on the scrapheap, derided, psychotic, prolific, angry. Lilith is highly placed in Van Gogh's chart, but it was blocked for many years by other planets and transits.

During the following months, as she traversed the sign of the Bull, and Jupiter the planet of plenty returned to Sagittarius, the place where it was when Van Gogh was born, the painter painted and painted, producing glory.

This moment in a person's life, in their mid-30s, when Jupiter and Lilith both return to the spot in the sky that they occupied at birth, can be incredibly productive, creative, expansive. Van Gogh shot himself as Lilith, by transit, exactly crossed his Ascendant. Perhaps her work was done.

into vines. What she touches multiplies.

Lilith in Taurus is potent, primal, powerful. My instinct is that this may be the strongest sign for her. Taurus is opposite Scorpio; both these signs are associated with sex and reproduction, passion and hunger. Taurus is physical, possessive. Taurus makes things that are real. Several of the people I work with who have Lilith in Taurus have an almost uncanny sexual allure, but in some individuals this also transmutes into great artistic ability, an ability to make material things come alive.

Lilith in Taurus

17 October 1905–12 July 1906
23 August 1914–18 May 1915
29 June 1923–23 March 1924
3 May 1932–27 June 1933
8 March 1941–2 December 1941
12 January 1950-8 October 1950
17 November 1958–14 August 1959
22 September 1967–18 June 1968
27 July 1976–27 April 1977
1 June 1985–27 February 1986
7 April 1994–2 January 1995
10 February 2003–7 November 2003
3 December 2011–12 September 2012
21 October 2020-18 July 2021
26 August 2029-23 May 2030

A couple of singers — from last century and this one— epitomise the sexual yearning of Lilith in Taurus. The great American singer Billie Holiday had Lilith in Taurus on her *Imum Coeli*, the part of her chart associated with foundations, home and family. The sign is associated traditionally with the throat and speech, and, of course, what made Holiday famous was her ability to sing of great heartbreak and loneliness. The very timbre of her voice was the blues. She seemed to express centuries of pain and abandonment. Maybe this came, at least partly, from her own unhappy Lilith-themed childhood: she was illegitimate and passed between carers, narrowly escaping rape aged 11. Her relationship with her own mother was close, yet troubled. But her voice also seems to come from deep in the collective.

Singer-songwriter Lana Del Rey is similarly famous for her tortured songs of relationships gone wrong. She also has this placement. It's empowered in her chart by a conjunction to Venus and the north node, a critical point in astrology. This is highly charged — Taurus being possibly the most undilutedly sexy sign. Her earthy, visceral lyrics describe being a woman who is also a creature with desires in the 21st century.

These powerful themes of desire and rejection may be something you experience yourself with this placement. The 19th century French poet Paul Verlaine, like Del Rey, has a conjunction of Venus and Lilith in Taurus, but in his case there's the added bonus of fiery Mars. His passionate, sordid affair with young Arthur Rimbaud scandalised Paris at the end of the 19th century. What the French term *nostalgie de la boue*, literally a nostalgia for mud, can be a feature of Lilith in Taurus. In English one might call that a love of the gutter, being drawn to the dregs, a desire to taste bitter effluence. That affair ended with a gun.

In terms of output another music master, JS Bach, also has Lilith in Taurus. Bach was incredibly prolific, turning out music that is still recognised as some of the most beautiful in the Western canon. Bach's feel for harmony and number, his deep spirituality and his exquisite sense of rhythm are all, perhaps, evident in other parts of his chart, but his Lilith in Taurus may be what gives his music a sensual, connected earthy hum.

Taurus is also a sign associated with consumption — food, drink, clothes. It can be gluttonous, or at least perceived as such. The French Queen Marie Antoinette, with Lilith in Taurus in her eleventh house of the people, had just this problem, which, of course, cost her her head. "Let them eat cake," was not the wisest thing to suggest to a hungry mob.

Peter Thiel, co-founder of PayPal, owner of Palantir and one of the richest men in the world, seems to have the insatiable hunger for more

Fleabag

In the mid-teens, a taboo-busting show about a sad, angry young woman broke all the rules of television sitcoms by putting Lilith in Taurus front and centre of a story.

It starred its creator Phoebe Waller Bridges, born with Lilith in Taurus. And the character she created, never named, but known as Fleabag, is a bundle of self-hatred and humour. Fleabag is consumed by guilt, desire, jealousy and an inability to conform to expectations. It's a show about how hard it is to navigate your 20s in the 21st century, about the reality of female sexual desire — and it is hilarious.

In fact, Waller Bridges has an opposition between Pluto, the Lord of the Underworld in sexy Scorpio, and Lilith in Taurus, a sign that appreciates a dirty joke.

that Lilith in Taurus can produce. His *Via Lamia* actually runs from pioneering Aries into Taurus, so he may have a powerful desire to both be first and have more — very useful qualities for a tech entrepreneur and investor. Other factors in his chart explain his actual success in achieving those ends, perhaps, but don't forget that Lilith is ruthless in her pursuit of fulfilment.

Some famous people with Lilith in Taurus

Vincent Van Gogh, Billie Holliday, Julie Christie, Susan Sontag, Nietzsche, Charlie Chaplin, Bob Dylan, Bernie Sanders, Chris Martin, Greta Garbo, Marie Antoinette, JS Bach, Gerard Manley Hopkins, Hilaire Belloc, Fernando Pessoa, John Berryman, Dylan Thomas, Bob Dylan, Anne Tyler, Manuel Puig, Anne Stevenson, Lana del Rey, Francis Bacon

Best: super-fertile and sexy
Worst: rolling in the gutter

Gemini

"every demon wants his pound of flesh
But I like to keep some things to myself"

— Florence Welch, 'Shake It Out'

"Whoever fights monsters should see to it that in the process he does not become a monster. And if you gaze long enough into an abyss, the abyss will gaze back into you."

— Friedrich Nietzsche

"I am fated to journey hand in hand with my strange heroes and to survey the surging immensity of life, to survey it through the laughter that all can see and through the tears unseen and unknown by anyone."

— Nikolai Gogol

"He's more myself than I am. Whatever our souls are made of, his and mine are the same."

— Emily Brontë, *Wuthering Heights*

"I have never let my schooling interfere with my education."

— Mark Twain

"All of us have to be prevaricators, hypocrites, and liars every day of our lives; otherwise the social structure would fall into pieces the first day. We must act in one another's presence just as we must wear clothes. It is for the best."

— O. Henry

"If it comes in one ear and it comes out immediately by the other, it's because, between the two, there is nothing to hold it."

— Georges Feydeau

"Desire makes everything blossom; possession makes everything wither and fade."

— Marcel Proust, *The Pleasures and The Days*

"Let us enrich ourselves with our mutual differences."

— Paul Valery

> "For women, the best aphrodisiacs are words. The G-spot is in the ears. He who looks for it below there is wasting his time."
>
> — Isabel Allende, *Of Love and Shadows*

Cast out of the garden, Lilith took to the air. Some say she sprouted leathery wings, others that they were feathered, like an angel. Her wild, true nature bore her up into the ether, and maybe, suddenly, she was able to look down on Eden, and see that it was just a garden, a contained space in a big world to explore.

The insatiable nature of Lilith can be expressed in Gemini through a kind of glorious, unquenchable curiosity: facts and more facts, data. There's also, often, a real flair with expression, and words can gain huge power coming from the pens or mouths of people with Lilith in Gemini. I have quite a few writers on my books with this placement, although sometimes Lilith in Gemini just likes to talk a lot. So, if you have Lilith in Gemini, do

Self portrait. Henri Fantin-Latour. Lilith in Gemini

watch what you say or write. It may have more impact than you imagine.

American President Abraham Lincoln is still regarded as one of the finest communicators ever to hold that office. His Gettysburg Address, a speech he made dedicated to the soldiers who fell at a terrible battle during the Civil War, epitomises Lilith in Gemini's facility with words. The speech is very short, yet it's resonated through the centuries. The words Lincoln chose were few yet directly to the point. It's notable that Lincoln's Lilith is directly on a critical angle of the chart of the United States.

Lilith in Gemini

12 July 1906–7April 1907
18 May 1915–10 February 1916
23 March 1924–16 December 1924
27 June 1933–21 October 1933
2 December 1941–27 August 1942
8 October 1950–3 July 1951
14 August 1959–8 May 1960
18 June 1968–14 March 1969
27 April 1977–17 January 1978
27 February 1986–23 November 1986
2 January 1995–29 September 1995
7 November 2003–3 August 2004
12 September 2012–9 June 2013
18 July 2021–14 April 2022
23 May 2030-18 February 2031

Lilith Returns: Wild Writing

The American writer Cheryl Strayed wrote about internal and external wilderness in her memoir *Wild: A Journey from Lost to Found*, which was subsequently made into a film starring Reese Witherspoon. She describes her years of addiction and squalor, and how she escaped by rediscovering the great wildness of America on a solo trek along the Pacific Crest Trail.

Strayed has Lilith in the storyteller's sign, Gemini, making an exact aspect to her nodal axis across Aries-Libra — the signs of the pioneer and the cultured city dweller, the hero and the lover. She becomes the hero of her own life when she embraces the wild and leaves behind people. The trek which changed her life took place in 1995, during one of her Lilith returns — that is when Lilith was back in Gemini. The book was published in 2012 and became a bestseller as Lilith was making her way back into Gemini for another return.

"I am Heathcliff"

That high-Victorian anti-hero Heathcliff is precisely an expression of the wild, dark energy, of Lilith conjured from the imagination of the writer Emily Bronte in her novel *Wuthering Heights.* Here is Heathcliff's beloved Catherine's description of him.

> *"...an unreclaimed creature, without refinement, without cultivation; an arid wilderness of furze and whinstone . . . Pray, don't imagine that he conceals depths of benevolence and affection beneath a stern exterior! He's not a rough diamond---a pearl-containing oyster of a rustic: he's a fierce, pitiless, wolfish man . . . and he'd crush you like a sparrow's egg."*

Emily Brontë was born with Lilith in Gemini, the sign of words and twins, in the seventh house of relationships and lovers, directly opposed by Neptune, the planet of imagination. *Wuthering Heights* unfolds as a series of stories within stories — centred around the destructive, obsessive love between Cathy and Heathcliff. These two are twinned by fate, pulled into a path that ruins themselves and the people around them. The action is set, of course, on the wild Yorkshire moors.

For Brontë, clearly the untamed part of herself was represented by a man. However, the twinning Gemini nature of this wildness is evident too — since it's both Heathcliff and Cathy who are too wild to be contained by society.

Civil war, battles between brothers, sibling rivalry: these are all the dark side of the sign of the twins. But this can be transmuted into something else — a great sporting rivalry. For example, tennis champion Rafael Nadal has a Sun-Lilith conjunction in Gemini. In fact, many great tennis players are born in Gemini, a sign known for swiftness, dexterity, hand-eye co-ordination, and doubling. Lilith gave Nadal that extra edge of persistence and ruthlessness. If he had not had to deal with Roger Federer's Moon-Lilith conjunction in Scorpio, another great sporting sign, he might have been top even more consistently.

As well as hands, Gemini is associated with mind, ideas and thoughts. Gemini is an intellectual sign, one of the air signs, and it sometimes shows a great hunger and fascination with ideas, or a very productive mind. I've people with multiple interests and talents with this placement, which is both exhilarating and confusing on occasion. Think of Gemini with many arms, like a Hindu goddess, juggling scissors.

When Lilith in Gemini goes wrong there can be just an overwhelming interior tangle. You might have negative voices nagging you, or persistent unhelpful thoughts, or just find yourself very easily distracted. The usefulness of astrology here is that once you recognise it as a phenomenon, you can start to steer another way. Use the Lilith in Gemini energy to give your words, or your hands extra power. The great boxer Muhammad Ali exemplified both those things. He used his facility with words to intimidate his opponents and the speed of his hands to knock them out.

A *Via Lamia*: About Jen

The Hollywood superstar Jennifer Aniston who became famous in the 1990s and remained on the A-list for 30 years was, for a time in the noughties, never off the front cover of gossip magazines. So much so that her talent as an actress was for a while eclipsed by a voracious appetite for details of her private life.

There were two main strands to the public 'Jen' story, both of which exemplify aspects of Lilith. The first was the break-up of her marriage to fellow actor Brad Pitt, who ran off with Angelina Jolie. This love triangle is a classic Lilith affair, with Jen cast in the role of rejected spouse. The second was her childlessness, raked over in the press.

You will be unsurprised to learn that Aniston has a wide *Via Lamia* running through the part of her chart associated with publicity and culminating at her Midheaven in Cancer, the place of highest public standing. It begins with mean Lilith in Gemini, the sign of pairs — and interestingly she and Pitt do look like they might be siblings — and ends with true Lilith in Cancer on the Midheaven.

Aniston is an example of how Lilith can be endearing. She is a beloved actress, who seems forever young, a Gemini attribute. In another chart, that Lilith placement could have made her quite reviled. For example, Yoko Ono was publicly blamed for breaking up the Beatles when she married John Lennon. Her Lilith in Gemini spans the same area as Aniston's but it does not reach into Cancer. Ono's life exemplifies another Lilith theme too. Ono's daughter Kyoko was stolen from her and disappeared for 23 years.

Sometimes Lilith can show us the way in which we diverge from the "norm". I've seen Lilith in Gemini with ADHD, for example. You may just want to know everything, touch everything, be everywhere. Focusing your ideas is important.

When you look at planets or points opposite the Sun or Venus, you can sometimes see a person's partner or attitude to partnership. French President Emmanuel Macron's partnership is famously unconventional. Macron is a super-Sagittarius, so much so that his style of leadership was often compared to that of Jupiter, King of the Gods — and ruler of Sagittarius. However, all that power in Sagittarius is balanced by Lilith in Gemini, the opposite sign. He married his teenage crush; she happened to be his already-married teacher, nearly 25 years older than he. It turned into a long marriage, and Brigitte Macron is said to be Emmanuel's secret weapon, telling him to stop talking so much, for instance. Macron is known for his Sagittarian verbosity. She was born with Lilith rising in that other sign of letters, Virgo.

Laura Bates, the English feminist who founded the Everyday Sexism project on twitter in 2012, has a Moon-Lilith-Chiron conjunction in Gemini, the journalist's sign. She launched the project on 16 April 2012, when Lilith was approaching an exact conjunction with Jupiter, the sign of growth.

Some famous people with Lilith in Gemini

Apollinaire, Arnold Wittgenstein, Arnold Toynbee, Jean Cocteau, Erle Stanley Gardner, William Faulkner, Marta Vergara, Bertolt Brecht, Hannah Arendt, John Dickson Carr, Laurens Van der Post, Paul McCartney, Alfred Lord Tennyson, Juliusz Slowacki, Karl Marx, Maurice Maeterlink, Theodore Dreiser, Susannah Clarke, Johanna Spyri,

Best: brilliant mind

Worst: lying tongue

Cancer

"You see, they have no judgment.
So it is natural that they should drown,
first the ice taking them in
and then, all winter, their wool scarves
floating behind them as they sink
until at last they are quiet.
And the pond lifts them in its manifold dark arms."

— Louise Gluck, 'The Drowned Children'

"I do not want my picture in your offices: the President is not an icon, an idol, or a portrait. Hang your kids' photos instead, and look at them each time you are making a decision."

— Volodymyr Zelensky

"People think I live in a cave and eat children."

— PJ Harvey

"You understand Teacher, don't you, that when you have a mother who's an angel and a father who is a cannibal king, and when you have sailed on the ocean all your whole life, then you don't know just how to behave in school with all the apples and ibexes."

— Astrid Lindgren, *Pippi Longstocking*

"Haven't laughed this hard in a long time
I better stop now before I start crying"

— Elliott Smith, 'Twilight'

In the sign of mothering and babies, moonshine and moods, you'd expect Lilith to pack quite a punch. And indeed she does.

When Lilith got to the desert, according to some yarns, she met a handsome demon called Samael, and became incredibly fecund. She gave birth to legions of demonettes every day, but every day legions of them died. The cycle of birth and death accelerated into a hurricane.

Lilith in Cancer may be both hugely fertile, or in absolute contrast, rejecting of children but fertile in other ways. There are several placements where Lilith may — but definitely not always — indicate childlessness or

Self portrait with Thorn Necklace and Hummingbird Frida Kahlo. Lilith in Cancer

trouble bearing children, and this is one of them. But thinking about my clients, I see quite a few parents with Lilith in Cancer. I have seen this placement in the charts of people that work with children who are in some way rejected by the system, for example, refugees or kids in care. I've also seen it in the charts of women who end up rescuing childlike men, in other words, whose mothering is diverted into relationships.

Lilith in Cancer

7 April 1907–3 January 1908
10 February 1916–7 November 1916
16 December 1924–12 September 1925
21 October 1933–18 July 1934
27 August 1942–24 May 1943
3 July 1951–28 March 1952
8 May 1960–31 January 1961
14 March 1969–7 December 1969
17 January 1978–12 October 1978
23 November 1986–18 August 1987
29 September 1995–23 June 1996
3 August 2004–28 April 2005
9 June 2013–4 March 2014
14 April 2022– 8 January 2023
18 February 2031–14 November 2031

Lilith in Cancer can, occasionally, suggest that your own experience of being mothered was erratic or unusual, or that your own mother was cast out for some reason. For example, there may be illegitimacy, or exile from the tribe for another reason.

Being cast out is not always as bad as it sounds. If you are forced to leave an oppressive community or even country, you may find yourself much happier in the new place. Lilith in Cancer can sometimes show up in the chart of a person who left their homeland and has lived life as an 'alien'.

Cancer is the sign associated with tribe and soil — both in the positive sense of being a 'family man or woman' and in the negative one of being a member of a mafia. The most famous mafioso of them all, Al Capone, has Lilith in Cancer.

Lilith never follows the rules. A notable Lilith in Cancer was Diana, Princess of Wales. She joined a mafia, the British royal family, disrupted it, and was cast out; a classic Lilith story. Indeed, she was also involved in a love triangle between her, Charles and Camilla. But then the archetype goes further. Diana was killed in an accident leaving behind two sons. For them, she became the lost mother. Interestingly, it is William, not Harry, who carries that scar most prominently astrologically. He has Lilith precisely on his Ascendant. Maybe he feels more rejected than we think.

There is an element of radical reform of the tribe in this placement too. Kemal Ataturk, nationalist founder of modern Turkey, who completely transformed his country, has Lilith in Cancer opposite his Capricorn Sun. Ataturk turned Turkey into a secular state, changing things from top to bottom, not least the alphabet. In his haste to change one nation, he accelerated history itself. It's interesting also that many of Ataturk's reforms were aimed at getting God out of government. He secularised the Turkish state — a reform that now seems impossibly 20th century.

Another notable political figure with this placement is Margaret Thatcher, Britain's first female prime minister, whose premiership reshaped the country. Both Thatcher and Ataturk shared radical visions, and both passionately believed they were caring for their citizens by destroying certain communities. There's a ruthlessness in here that feels very Lilith.

Creatrix and Lover

Mexican artist Frida Kahlo was born when a stunning line up of planets gathered across Gemini and Cancer. Led by Venus and Pluto in Gemini, Lilith, Neptune, the Sun, Jupiter and the North Node of the Moon were all in the sensitive, watery sign of the Crab.

Lilith is right in the middle of that spread of planets, very close to Neptune and the Sun, and her life unfolded with powerfully Lilith themes. She was, first of all, a prolific creator. About 140 of her paintings survive, but her artistic verve spilled over into the creation of her home, La Casa Azul, and into her use of her own self — through jewellery, clothing and multiple self-portraits as muse.

As well as that creative flow, Kahlo's life was Lilithian in other ways. She had several miscarriages, possibly because of a terrible accident as a young woman, which damaged her reproductive organs. In her natal chart Uranus, the planet of accidents, is directly opposite Lilith and conjoins Mars, which sometimes symbolises violence.

On the day of her marriage to fellow artist Diego Rivera, Lilith was, by transit, conjoining Uranus and opposing herself. So perhaps it was inevitable that Rivera and Kahlo's marriage also exemplified that Lilith theme of three-way relationships. There seems always to have been at least one other party involved in their marriage. Both partners had multiple affairs. This tumultuous partnership was on and off until her early death at the age of 47 under a conjunction of Saturn, the grim reaper himself, and Lilith in Scorpio, the sign of the underworld. On that day, Pluto, ruler of Scorpio was directly on Kahlo's ascendant, and Mercury Retrograde was conjoining her natal Lilith.

Some famous people with Lilith in Cancer

Kesha, Jennifer Aniston, Robin Williams, Jimi Hendrix, Mick Jagger, Kobe Bryant, Jean-Luc Melenchon, Novak Djokovic, Janis Joplin, Hugh Grant, Margaret Thatcher, Rimbaud, Malcolm X, Ataturk, Oscar Wilde, Amal Clooney, Queen Victoria, Swami Vivekenanda, Jean-Michel Basquiat, Diana, Princess of Wales, Carlos Castaneda, Carl Sagan, Gregory Peck, James Stewart, Elliot Smith, Rama Krishna, Brian Wilson

Best: mother of millions
Worst: imperialistic vision

Leo

"The eyes of others our prisons; their thoughts our cages."

— Virginia Woolf

"No woman should be authorised to stay at home and raise her children. Society should be totally different. Women should not have that choice, precisely because if there is such a choice, too many women will make that one."

— Simone de Beauvoir

"Mothers of America
let your kids go to the movies!
Get them out of the house so they won't know what you're up to
it's true that fresh air is good for the body
but what about the soul
that grows in darkness, embossed by silvery images
and when you grow old as grow old you must
they won't hate you
they won't criticise you they won't know
they'll be in some glamorous country
they first saw on a Saturday afternoon or playing hookey
they may even be grateful to you
for their first sexual experience
which only cost you a quarter."

— Frank O'Hara, 'Ave Maria'

"What Is Love? I have met in the streets a very poor young man who was in love. His hat was old, his coat worn, the water passed through his shoes and the stars through his soul."

— Victor Hugo, *Les Misérables*

"One narcissus among the ordinary beautiful
flowers, one unlike all the others!
on his glittering terrible
carriage, he claimed his due.
It is finished. No one had heard her.
No one! She had strayed from the herd."

— Rita Dove, 'Persephone Falling'

Unfinished self portrait. Egon Schiele. Lilith in Leo

"We could never have loved the earth so well if we had had no childhood in it, if it were not the earth where the same flowers come up again every spring that we used to gather with our tiny fingers as we sat lisping to ourselves on the grass, the same hips and haws on the autumn hedgerows, the same redbreasts that we used to call 'God's birds' because they did no harm to the precious crops. What novelty is worth that sweet monotony where everything is known and loved because it is known?"

— George Eliot, *The Mill on the Floss*

Oh the glory of Lilith in the sign of the Sun, the heart of creation. In the legend of Lilith, she gives birth to endless babies. This fertility can be read in another way though, as endless creativity, the flow of the Kundalini, the dark feminine energy. Tapping into this aspect of Lilith may produce endless children of the mind, hand or heart. This is why you often see a powerful Lilith in the charts of exceptionally prolific and inventive artists.

Lilith in Leo

3 January 1908–29 September 1908
7 November 1916–4 August 1917
12 September 1925–10 June 1926
18 July 1934–15 April 1935
24 May 1943–18 February 1944
28 March 1952–24 December 1952
31 January 1961–29 October 1961
7 December 1969–3 September 1970
12 October 1979–9 July1979
18 August 1987–13 May 1988
23 June 1996–19 March 1997
28 April 2005–22 January 2006
4 March 201–27 November 2014
8 January 2023 –3 October 2023
14 November 2031–8 August 2032

Here are two 20th century examples. The Spanish painter Pablo Picasso was a dominant figure in the art world from early in the century. This was in part due to his endless creativity — he painted, he potted, he sculpted, he drew, he squiggled and splashed. He was like this from childhood to the very end of his life at 91 years old. Picasso was born with Lilith rising in Leo.

Agatha Christie, one of the 20th century's most prolific writers, was born with Lilith in Leo in the eighth house (mysteries and death) exactly trining the action planet Mars on her Ascendant and making a perfect aspect to her Midheaven (fame).

Tapping into this effortless output may also be what Jung was referring to when he wrote about the creative power of the dark feminine. He, of course, was writing as if the male and female experiences are entirely different, whereas in fact, for a woman, the creative power of Lilith may be just as powerful. This is the libido, the sex drive, the creative energy which can be poured into art or sexual adventure or both. The Spanish painter Picasso is a super example of this — a randy old goat until deep into old age.

Numerous creatives have Lilith in Leo, and one of the attributes of Leo is originality, or uniqueness. So Lilith can lend you a fluent, productive creative originality. Leo is also the sign of children, and I have seen Lilith in Leo in the charts of both people with many children, and none.

Lilith in Leo can also bring notable theatrical charisma: Barack Obama, Jimmy Page, Jim Morrison — and just sheer talent — Joni Mitchell, Virginia Woolf.

The symbolism is interesting. Leo is the brightest sign, ruled as it is by the Sun, the burning fire at the heart of our own solar system. It creates life. It is the vital force. Yet Lilith is a black void, an empty space, a mathematical notion; something you can never see. This is why a Sun-Lilith conjunction can be a very strange combination with which to live. I have several friends with this one, perhaps because I like the otherness and witchery of it. And one thing all have in common is an endless creativity,

Guitar Queen

The legendary singer-songwriter Joni Mitchell was born with a fantastic conjunction of Lilith and Jupiter in her ninth house, close to her Midheaven, the place of career, status and the way in which the public sees you. It's not unusual to see expansive Jupiter in this position for performers.

Mitchell was a unique musician. For example, she is a famously inventive guitarist, tuning her instruments in her own way that creates a truly original sound. The way she flexes and extends her voice, swooping and wailing, is also unique, and often sounds otherworldly; indeed she sounds as if she is singing on the very edge of the desert shoreline into the wind.

One of her many, many lovely Lilith lines is in the song 'Green', where she exhorts a little child to be a non-conformist. This particular song was about her own Lilith story when she was forced to put her baby up for adoption eight months after the child was born.

This was when Lilith was making an exact conjunction to her South Node — the place of release, opposite to her stellium in Leo — Lilith, Jupiter, north node, Pluto. In fact, Mitchell has said that this incredibly painful moment in her life is what catapulted her into her career. You can see this in that powerful opposition. She wrote songs and performed out of the sadness. When at last she was reunited with her daughter in 1997, Lilith returned to Leo. For many years after this, Mitchell was too contented to write or perform: a circle had completed. Her Lilith story had reached a happy ending.

whether for actually making things, or ideas, or producing children. But there is also a dark side.

Lilith in Leo can lend an extraordinary dark charisma, and a hunger for controlling others. It can be bossy, and if the bossiness doesn't work, manipulative. I've seen Lilith in Leo people change the atmosphere in a room from sunny to thunderous. Russian President Vladimir Putin has an incredible Lilith placement, which explains his ruthless grip on power. Lilith is in Leo precisely on his Midheaven, the most public face of your chart. He is a king, Leo, and he will stop at nothing, Lilith.

It's important to know your own power — and powerlessness — with this placement. This charisma can also lead to being cast out or rejected in the classic Lilith manner. I have seen people who have been thrown out of their own families, rejected by their own children, or who have been forced to leave to retain their own identity, with this placement.

Philosopher Queen

Philosopher Simone de Beauvoir, author of *The Second Sex*, one of the foundational texts of modern feminism, was born with Mean Lilith at 0° Leo, making a perfect trine to her Sagittarius Ascendant. Sagittarius is the philosopher's sign. She demonstrated her own philosophy in the way she lived her life, free from convention. Her *Via Lamia* runs from Leo to Cancer, the sign of mothers. Mean Lilith makes an out-of-sign trine to her Moon at 29° Pisces, thus creating a Grand Trine pattern in de Beauvoir's chart. Her attitude to mothering was unusual. She did not seem to think it was particularly valuable.

De Beauvoir was one of the activists who forced the French government to legalise abortion, a Lilith concern, in the early 1970s.

On a completely different note, although connected via Lilith themes, de Beauvoir's attitude to other women's sexual safety and in general to children seems to have come secondary to ideas about sexual liberation. This lack of sexual boundaries is a Lilith theme, and it's notable that de Beauvoir's Lilith is in her eighth house which is literally associated with sex and sexuality. Leo is the sign associated with children and playing. She was suspended from teaching for seducing and grooming her pupils. In 1977, she signed a petition to remove the age of consent in France.

With Lilith in Leo, you must honour your own uniqueness, individuality and possibly talent. Your creative energy may be burning to come out and you need to give it an outlet. You don't have to be Virginia Woolf or Leonard Cohen, but you do need to find a way to express that inner wildness in a creative way. This may be through cooking or dancing or singing to yourself in the bath, but let it flow.

Lilith in Leo can burn very brightly, and too fast. You need to learn to steady the pace and not use up all of your precious Leo divinity too soon, like Jim Morrison of The Doors, who died at 27.

But speaking of longevity, Queen Elizabeth II, the longest serving British monarch ever, was born with Lilith in Leo, which is, of course, the sign of royalty, and there may be a touch of royalty about you too. Lilith, in one of her guises, is, of course, the queen of the underworld. Which makes one think a little about Elizabeth Windsor…

Finally, there can be a humanitarian aspect to this placement. Remember that Leo is opposite Aquarius, the sign of the common people. Lilith here may be looking across the zodiac, regarding the people, either benignly or with rage.

Some famous people with Lilith in Leo

George Eliot, Alfred Hitchock, Hugh Hefner, Vladimir Nabokov, Rita Dove, Barack Obama, Marilyn Monroe, Rihanna, Vladimir Putin, George Clooney, John F Kennedy, Catherine Zeta Jones, Elizabeth II, Isaac Newton, Jim Morrison, George Harrison, Lorde, Sophia Loren, Frederic Chopin, Jimmy Page, Leonard Cohen, Ernest Hemingway, Agatha Christie, Franklin D Roosevelt, Joni Mitchell, Virginia Woolf, Francoise Sagan, Marquis de Sade, Jules Verne, Rebecca Solnit

Best: unbridled originality
Worst: untamed ego

Virgo

"You only have to let the soft animal of your body
love what it loves."

— Mary Oliver, 'Wild Geese'

"When people say that nothing happens in their lives I believe them. But you must understand that everything happens to an artist; time is always redeemed, nothing is lost and wonders never cease."

— Muriel Spark, *Loitering with Intent*

"Hands that serve are holier than lips that pray."

— Sai Baba

"We realize the importance of our voices only when we are silenced."

— Malala Yousafzai

"We do not have to visit a madhouse to find disordered minds; our planet is the mental institution of the universe."

— Johann Wolfgang von Goethe

Self portrait. Henry Fuseli. Lilith in Virgo

> "The corporate revolution will collapse if we refuse to buy what they are selling – their ideas, their version of history, their wars, their weapons, their notion of inevitability.
> Remember this: We be many and they be few. They need us more than we need them.
> Another world is not only possible, she is on her way. On a quiet day, I can hear her breathing."
>
> — Arundhati Roy, *War Talk*

> "Vegan food is soul food in its truest form. Soul food means to feed the soul. And, to me, your soul is your intent. If your intent is pure, you are pure."
>
> — Erykah Badu

We arrive at Virgo, the sixth sign ruled by Mercury. Virgo is a sign of some complexity, as you may be able to understand simply by pondering its quality and element — mutability and earth. When is earth itself mutable? And then if you consider the god Mercury himself, we come to another question: how can an earth sign be ruled by the god of speed?

The symbol for Virgo is a woman carrying a sheaf of wheat, like the double goddess of the corn herself, Demeter/Persephone; and here we are at the end of summer, turning into the next season, celebrating the abundance of nature. This is the mutable earth, the change of season. And Mercury is the god of mind as well as speed, and in much of the world this is the beginning of the new scholastic year, back to school, a time of sharpening pencils and fresh new stationery.

Virgo is associated with writers and craftspeople; the meticulous, the editorial. And if you have this placement, you may find that you are prolific either as writer or maker.

If you have Lilith in Virgo, you may have a deep love of wildness, whether it is the heart of a flower in the city, or a dripping woodland. This could, for some of you, feel almost like a craving, a desire that is visceral. You feel drawn to some kind of oblivion in nature, losing yourself regarding the canopy of the forest, or the rush of the tide.

Perhaps it's no surprise then that one of this century's greatest nature poets, Mary Oliver, was born with Lilith in the heart of her Virgo Sun. Oliver's poems are beautifully balanced and structured; they celebrate wilderness, a thing of Lilith, and biological life itself. Another great lover of nature was John Muir, founder of America's Sierra Club, passionate campaigner for America's glorious great parks, defender of nature, walker, writer. He came over from Scotland to the United States and fell in love with the wide open spaces, the high mountains, the clear streams and the cathedrals of redwood. He was born with Lilith in earthy Virgo, the sign of writers and gardeners, opposite Venus in Pisces, the sign of the mystic. It was his eloquence that moved the public and establishment to see and cherish America's natural beauty — and his Lilith is also in the house of communications making a conjunction with Jupiter, the planet of large: those parks are vast.

Lilith in Virgo

29 September 1908–23 June 1909
4 August 1917–29 April 1918
10 June 1926–5 March 1927
15 April 1935–9 January 1936
18 February 1944–14 November 1944
24 December 1952–19 September 1953
29 October 1961–26 July 1962
3 September 1970–31 May 1971
9 July1979–5 April 1980
13 May 1988–8 February 1989
19 March 1997–14 December 1997
22 January 2006–20 October 2006
27 November 2014–25 August 2015
3 October 2023–29 June 2024
8 August 2032–4 May 2033

Along with a profound connection with the natural world, mysticism seems to be a common feature of Lilith in Virgo. Remember that she is looking across at the most numinous sign of them all, Pisces, the place of unfathomable depth.

That most influential and beloved European author, Johann Wolfgang von Goethe, was born with Lilith in Virgo. One of his most famous novels, *The Sorrows of Young Werther*, is about a man who falls in love with someone who does not reciprocate his desire. And this may be quite a Lilith in Virgo experience — a love for something, or someone who is as unknowable as the ocean itself, or who reflects your self back at you like a mirror.

Virgo is also one of the signs associated with mind, and if you have Lilith here you may have scrambled, crazy thoughts, or you may find that your thinking is extraordinarily original. Or that Lilith events greatly

Philosophical Anorexia

Frail, mystical, fiercely intelligent Simone Weil was born with a classic philosopher's combination of an Aquarian Sun and Sagittarius Rising. These are the signs of big systems of thought. But her Lilith-Jupiter conjunction in Virgo shows what those big ideas were about: service, self-denial, rootedness, work. Those are all Virgoan themes.

Her most influential book was called in English *The Need for Roots*, and in French *L'Enracinement, prélude à une déclaration des devoirs envers l'être humain* which translates literally as *Rootedness, an introduction to a declaration of the duties towards the human being*. It is an extremely original work that is still influential today. She was also deeply mystical, having first-hand experience of the numinous and close personal identification with Christ.

Her own self-denial also has themes of Lilith in Virgo, exaggerated by the conjunction with Jupiter, the chart ruler. It's a matter of debate whether she starved herself to death at the age of 34 out of sympathy for occupied Europe, but it is certain that she was repulsed by her own body, referring to her 'disgustingness'.

influence your art or your thinking. These may be connected with nature, or untamed sexuality, or the dark side of parenting.

Nobel prize winning author Herta Muller's work addresses specific Lilith themes of exile. She was born into the German-speaking minority in Romania under communist rule. Many members of her community were shipped off as slave labour into the Russian gulags, and her most famous book *The Hunger Angel* describes that experience from first-hand interviews. The Hunger Angel itself is an extraordinary evocation of Lilith in Virgo. The Hunger Angel is the feeling of near starvation itself, which is so painful that it actually keeps you alive. This touches on a basic theme of Lilith in Virgo — the opposite of the abundance of the season, that is lack or even starvation. I have seen this placement in the charts of clients with anorexia, although I've also seen many charts with Lilith in Virgo with no such problem. Self-denial can also happen sometimes with Lilith making a conjunction to the Sun.

Some famous people with Lilith in Virgo

Pink , Adam Levine, Francoise Hardy, Victor Hugo, Alfred Hitchcock, Erykah Badu, Michelangelo, Fidel Castro, Herta Muller, Dalai Lama , Indira Ghandi, Tom Cruise, Sigmund Freud

Best: outrageously brilliant wordsmith

Worst: disordered body image

Shima Seien, *Mudai [Untitled]*. Lilith in Libra

Libra

"The beautiful is always bizarre."

— Charles Baudelaire

"It's like in the great stories, Mr. Frodo. The ones that really mattered. Full of darkness and danger they were. And sometimes you didn't want to know the end… because how could the end be happy? How could the world go back to the way it was when so much bad had happened? But in the end, it's only a passing thing… this shadow. Even darkness must pass."

— J.R.R. Tolkien, *The Two Towers*

"Most reckless things are beautiful in some way, and recklessness is what makes experimental art beautiful, just as religions are beautiful because of the strong possibilities that they are founded on nothing."

— John Ashbery

"Because men are killing the forests the fairy tales are running away."

— Günter Grasse, *Rat*

"Good God, if our civilization were to sober up for a couple of days, it'd die of remorse on the third—"

— Malcolm Lowry, *Under the Volcano*

"Where you used to be, there is a hole in the world, which I find myself constantly walking around in the daytime, and falling in at night. I miss you like hell."

— Edna St. Vincent Millay

Marriage, beauty, balance, justice — these are all themes that become extreme with Lilith in Libra. These are where you break rules, breach boundaries, ignore convention, and in the process, you may create something new.

Libra is an air sign, therefore one of the signs concerned with human-to-human interactions. Specifically, Libra is about our peers, our one-to-ones. Lilith in Libra can show that we learn about the wildness through partnerships. I've seen this placement frequently with people who marry outside the tribe, simply someone their parents would never, ever have chosen.

Lilith in Libra

18 August 1900–14 May 1901
23 June 1909–19 March 1910
29 April 1918–23 January 1919
March 1927–28 November 1927
9 January 1936–3 October 1936
14 November 1944–8 August 1945
19 September 1953–14 June 1954
26 July 1962–20 April 1963
31 May 1971–24 February 1972
5 April 1980–30 December 1980
8 February 1989–4 November 1989
14 December 1997–10 September 1998
20 October 2006–17 July 2007
25 August 2015–21 May 2016
29 June 2024–27 March 2025
4 May 2033-30 June 2034

That's often a really lovely way this Lilith is expressed. Sometimes that person is much older or younger, a different religion or nationality. This relationship is likely to be something that expands your horizons or helps you explore your own wild nature.

On the other hand, you may find yourself attracted to people who are really unhinged, irrational, or just plain crazy. If so, you're not stuck with this pattern, but it is worth asking yourself if it is a pattern and then questioning how it is that you behave within relationships, because this could also be true. You may be peachy on the outside when you're dealing with other people, but when you come home, the Lilith comes out.

Entrepreneur, DOGE supremo, breaker of institutions, Elon Musk has Lilith in Libra, the sign of relationships, an area of life where Musk has certainly behaved in a non-conformist manner. It's also the sign of beauty, of course, and Musk has had plenty of surgery to change the way he looks to conform with his own ideas of attractiveness. His sometime wife Grimes — a notably Lilith kind of tag — has Lilith on her Midheaven. No wonder he was attracted for a while. Libra is also the sign associated with legislation, so it's notable that Musk's arrival in the White House in 2025 was a legal bonfire.

One way of controlling your own Lilith in Libra is to have a person, or several people, with whom you do your Lilith on a one-to-one basis. For example, you might have a partner that you travel with to exotic cities, or a hairdresser who makes you look extraordinary once a week

Libra is one of the fashion signs, and Lilith here can simply mean you have an outrageous talent with dressing up — or down. While a Sun Libra may always look elegant, Lilith in Libra looks like the queen of the night. The inventor of the Little Black Dress, Coco Chanel, was born with an extraordinary Lilith-north node conjunction directly on her Midheaven. Her destiny was always to express Lilith to the greater world — and she did this in two very Libran ways — through fashion, and collaborating with the Nazis. Chanel's politics were ultra-nationalist and elitist before the war, so perhaps it was no surprise that she worked with the occupiers. Chanel leveraged her status as an Aryan during the war to wrest control of her business from her investors, a Jewish family called Wertheimer.

Chanel is an interesting example, because Libra is often a deeply political sign, a sign about taking sides, joining a party, being in an 'in group', and Chanel powerfully exemplified this in her relationship to European aristocracy within which, although she was far from aristocratic herself, she had established alliances from the very start of her career. For example, British Prime Minister and hereditary peer Winston Churchill intervened after the war to protect her from being tried for collaboration.

Women's Rights

Mary Wollstonecraft, author of *A Vindication of the Rights of Women*, and mother of *Frankenstein* author Mary Shelley has Lilith in the sign of justice and fairness, Libra. It's on a critical point in the chart, known as 'the bendings', a point half-way between her Nodes in Capricorn, the sign of the patriarchy, and Cancer, the sign of motherhood. You might make something of the fact that Wollstonecraft died in childbirth, crucified on a cross of motherhood and patriarchy.

Another well-known feminist voice, Gisele Halimi, who founded *Choisir*, the pressure group which forced the French government to legalise abortion, has Lilith in the same position, appropriately for a lawyer, in Libra, which is the sign of justice and law. Halimi came to prominence defending the signatories of "*The Manifesto of the 343 Sluts*", published in 1971 on a conjunction of Lilith and Pluto in Virgo. *The Manifesto*, written by Simone de Beauvoir, was signed by prominent French women, who had all had illegal abortions. It was a truly Lilith-style event.

Just in case Chanel is depressing you, here's a really heroic Lilith in Libra. Anti-apartheid leader Nelson Mandela spent a lifetime fighting for equality. His Lilith in Libra conjoins Mars, the warrior. Now there's a story of a person thrown out of society and reborn back into it.

This is a sign ruled by Venus, the planet of beauty but also harmony, and it is symbolised by the scales. It's a sign connected with law and justice. The scales may be one of the most commonly used astrological signs seen outside every courtroom across the world. I've come across Libran Liliths whose work has been about rebalancing those scales, taking on cases that seemed impossible, defending the defenceless, righting outrageous wrongs. You may find yourself, like one Libran Lilith on my books, working in a women's shelter, or fighting your way through the courts in a prolonged divorce.

Since Libra is Venus ruled, your Lilith may either take out your anger on women, or put you in the role of victim because of your femaleness.

Some famous people with Lilith in Libra

Ingmar Bergman, Simone Weil, Kim Kardashian, Elon Musk, Alain Delon, Robert Redford, Ryan Gosling, RD Laing, Oprah Winfrey, Nikola Tesla, Demi Moore, Bob Marley, Nelson Mandela, Quentin Tarantino, Coco Chanel, Recep Tayyip Erdogan, Benito Mussolini, Justin Trudeau, Franz Kafka

Best: unbounded artistic vision
Worst: creator of false masks

Scorpio

"Courage is the most important of all the virtues because without courage, you can't practice any other virtue consistently."

— Maya Angelou

"Beauty is terror. Whatever we call beautiful, we quiver before it."

— Donna Tartt, *The Secret History*

"What are heavy? sea-sand and sorrow.
What are brief? today and tomorrow.
What are frail? spring blossoms and youth.
What are deep? the ocean and truth."

— Christina Rossetti, 'What Are Heavy?'

"I'm nobody! Who are you?
Are you nobody, too?
Then there's a pair of us—don't tell!
They'd banish us, you know.

How dreary to be somebody!
How public, like a frog
To tell your name the livelong day
To an admiring bog!"

— Emily Dickinson

"I'm always happy when I'm surrounded by water, I think I'm a mermaid or I was a mermaid.

The ocean makes me feel really small and it makes me put my whole life into perspective."

— Beyoncé Knowles

You can see that there might be a natural affinity between wild, untamed Lilith and Scorpio, the survivor. Scorpio has a reputation for being able to die and come back to life, to self-destruct like a phoenix and rise from the ashes.

The survival instinct of Scorpio is fierce, resourceful, and overpowering. When combined with the bounds-breaking of Lilith, you can find

Self portrait. Clara von Rappard. Lilith in Scorpio

yourself with an unstoppable will to live, to find security and sometimes to go to the edge. Or you may find yourself writing endless break-up songs, like Taylor Swift, surely the queen of the genre.

In life, you may find yourself pushed to survive — this may be through personal or collective trauma. It's notable that British prime minister Winston Churchill, with Lilith in Scorpio, was very successful in wartime, but a failure as a politician during peacetime. This ability to look into the wild darkness, survive and report back may lead you to work on the edges of life — in the emergency ward or hospice, for example.

Lilith in Scorpio

14 May 1901–9 February 1902
19 March 1910–15 December 1910
23 January 1919–20 October 1919
28 November 1927–24 August 1928
3 October 1936–29 June 1937
8 August 1945–5 May 1946
14 June 1954–10 March 1955
20 April 1963–13 January 1964
24 February 1972–18 November 1972
30 December 1980–24 September 1981
4 November 1989–30 July 1990
10 September 1998–5 June 1999
17 July 2007–10 April 2008
21 May 2016–14 February 2017
27 March 2025–20 December 2025
30 January 2034-26 October 2034

People with Lilith in Scorpio can often find huge inner resources, going not just the extra mile, but the extra seven-leagues. Many actors who bring an unnerving level of intensity to their performances have the secret inner resource of Lilith in Scorpio — Winona Ryder, Ralph Fiennes, Kristen Stewart.

This intense ability to focus can fuel worldly ambition, of course, or spiritual growth. Pope Francis had Lilith in Scorpio. His first encyclical was entitled *The Earth, Our Sister, Cries Out*. It was a call for us to stop polluting the planet. In astrology, it's important to look at pairs of signs in opposition. Scorpio, hell, is opposite Taurus, Eden. The Pope was looking at Eden from the place of his Lilith, queen of hell. Pollution and corruption are concerns of Lilith — either for or against.

Scorpio is also a generative sign. They make life, plant the seed and can create resources. Both Beyoncé Knowles and Taylor Swift, arguably the two most financially successful American pop stars of the first quarter of the 21st century, have Lilith in Scorpio. There are many other factors in their success, but their ability to generate huge amounts of money may be a feature of Lilith in Scorpio.

Scorpio, along with Taurus is a money sign, but Scorpio tends to be more about wealth than salary. A couple of the founders of the tech gazillionaires club, Steve Jobs and Jeff Bezos, have Lilith in Scorpio, signifying a limitless capacity to generate wealth. Mind you, Lilith can also show us a place of insatiable hunger. Will Bezos ever have enough money? Did Jobs? Interestingly, Jobs was well-known for starving his body — at one point his diet was a single apple a day — while increasing the contents of his wallet. This opposition between the Eden of Taurus and the asceticism of Scorpio. Peter Thiel, another member of the club, has his Lilith in Taurus.

Rotten to the Core

Movie-maker David Lynch was fascinated by the teeming life that lies under the rock of suburban America. Lynch was born with Lilith precisely conjoining his Ascendant. This placement is like seeing the world through Lilith sunglasses.

Scorpio rising certainly can see the world 'through a glass darkly' and Lynch's vision has a specifically Lilithian slant.

His voyeuristic vision included many versions of the archetype — from the sultry singer played by Isabella Rossellini in the film *Blue Velvet* to the entire female cast of his hugely influential TV series *Twin Peaks*, first aired in 1990. All the female characters in the show represent some form of Lilith, from Audrey Horne, irresistible seductress to murder victim Laura Palmer.

Scorpio is, of course, looking directly across at luscious, fecund Taurus. The actresses in Lynch's films and TV shows were all similarly gorgeous. I think many would argue, including me, that Lynch's vision was profoundly misogynistic. The hunger for flesh, the punishment inflicted on the women, and the pornographic rapes were all clothed in art house mystique. Make your own decision about them, but you can be certain that these are Lilith visions. To me, this is Lilith at her saddest and most sordid.

None of these people started with absolutely nothing mind you, and both Swift and Knowles came from families with real financial nous. What Lilith adds is the boundary-breaking nature.

Personally, be warned that this can go in exactly the opposite direction, because Scorpio placements can also pull us into debt, depending on other parts of the chart.

Scorpio has a reputation as the sexiest sign in the zodiac, so you can see that Lilith here might lead to unbounded sexual appetite or experimentation, a sense of unlimited possibility. Sex might become a means of escape or transcendence.

The Apple and the Snake

In many medieval depictions of Lilith, she is shown as the snake offering Eve the apple from the tree of knowledge. Indeed, she often has exactly the same head as Eve, with a snake's body, as if she is a double or a reflection.

This peculiar angle on the Bible story offers a glimpse into some other possible interpretations of the myth of the Garden of Eden. It was a subject chewed over by both Jewish and Christian scholars. In some interpretations, the tree of life becomes the tree of death, for example. Eating the apple from the Tree of Knowledge is what causes Adam and Eve to lose their immortality and be cast out of the Garden of Eden.

In this, they are following in the footsteps of Adam's first wife Lilith, who has already made a home in the great world. But whereas she, being simply cast out because she will not obey her husband, actually remains immortal, they are doomed to die, work and suffer the pain of being human.

The serpent is sometimes associated with the sign Scorpio, as is knowledge of death. It's interesting to speculate about Steve Jobs, the founder of Apple Computers, who was obsessed with the fruit itself. Jobs was born with Lilith, indeed his entire Via Lamia, in Scorpio. Is the modern "Apple", a fruit from the Tree of Knowledge? Offered to us by a snake in the form of Jobs, dressed as he always was in a black turtle neck. Just a thought.

Some famous people with Lilith in Scorpio

Steve Jobs, Taylor Swift, Jeff Bezos, Angela Merkel, Winston Churchill, Björk, Marlene Dietrich, Gwyneth Paltrow, Johnny Depp, Beyoncé Knowles, Emma Watson, Natalie Portman, Kristen Stewart, Pope Francis, Roger Federer, Serge Gainsbourg, Walt Disney, Fyodor Dostoyevsky, Stanley Kubrick, Brad Pitt

Best: creator of abundance

Worst: always hungry

Fatally Funny

If you're the second sex, or in some other way weaker than the masters who rule society, one of your weapons is humour. You can always laugh at your oppressors. Lilith herself was said to tickle the soles of babies' feet and make them smile.

Baubo was the Greek goddess of mirth and the only person who could make Demeter laugh when she was mourning her daughter Persephone's disappearance. Thus having a belly laugh became an essential part of the Eleusinian mysteries. Dirty jokes in particular were — allegedly — encouraged.

The queen of such things in cinema was, of course, the raunchy music hall artiste, Mae West, who was born with a conjunction of Lilith and Uranus, the planet of surprises in Scorpio, the sign of sex.

Sagittarius

"I am not what happened to me, I am what I choose to become."
— Carl Gustav Jung

"Art is the mirror of our betrayed ideals."
— Doris Lessing, *The Golden Notebook*

"What writes history is the power of ideas. And every moment offers the potential to write something new."
— Helena Blavatsky

"The joy of life consists in the exercise of one's energies, continual growth, constant change, the enjoyment of every new experience. To stop means simply to die. The eternal mistake of mankind is to set up an attainable ideal."
— Aleister Crowley

"You don't get rich writing science fiction. If you want to get rich, you start a religion."
— L. Ron Hubbard

"I am a forest fire
And I am the forest
And I am the fire
And I am a witness
watching it."
— Mitski, 'A Burning Hill'

"A revolution is not a dinner party, or writing an essay, or painting a picture, or doing embroidery; it cannot be so refined, so leisurely and gentle, so temperate, kind, courteous, restrained and magnanimous. A revolution is an insurrection, an act of violence by which one class overthrows another."
— Mao Tse-tung

Lilith in Sagittarius

9 February 1902–5 November 1902
15 December 1910–11 September 1911
20 October 1919–19 July 1920
24 August 1928–22 May 1929
29 June 1937–27 March 1938
5 May 1946–30 January 1947
10 March 1955–6 December 1955
3 January 1964–10 October 1964
18 November 1972–15 August 1973
24 September 1981–20 June 1982
30 July 1990–25 April 1991
5 June 1999–29 February 2000
10 April 2008–3 January 2009
14 February 2017–9 November 2017
20 December 2025–14 September 2026
26 October 2034–21 July 2035

Self portrait. Zinaida Serebriakova. Lilith in Sagittarius

"The supreme madness is to see life as it is and not as it should be."
— Jacques Brel

When the queen of untamed nature enters the land of the centaur, you can imagine that anything becomes possible, even starting your own religion.

Sagittarius is a sign of boundlessness, wilderness and wildness, so it already sounds like a description of the place where Lilith lives. After going through the dark of Scorpio, she emerges into a fiery place where she can expand and run free. All knowledge is possible. Knowledge is power.

Sagittarius is associated with philosophy and religion — big, all embracing ideas and systems of knowledge. Lilith here can be fantastically,

The Beast

Aleister Crowley, the 20th century's most reviled black magician, creator of the Thoth tarot, occult practitioner and late resident of Hastings, has Lilith in a fiery Grand Trine with the north node and the Ascendant — all at precisely 8°.

Lilith is in his fifth house, the place of theatre and children, in Sagittarius, the sign of organised religion and priests. Crowley was a notorious showman and show-off, infamous in his lifetime, known as The Great Beast 666 and labelled 'the wickedest man in the world'. The tabloid newspapers loved reporting on his shenanigans.

Sagittarius is, of course, also the sign of the guru, a role that Crowley embraced, and the lover of wisdom, and he was certainly widely read and extremely prolific in his own writings, synthesising esoteric traditions from different cultures. This interest in many cultures is certainly a Sagittarius theme, as is the publishing history. One of Crowley's daughters, who died in childhood, was named Lilith.

intellectually daring. You have only to look at a short list of famous thinkers with this placement to see that the wilder shores of intellect are a really powerful place for Lilith. These folks all have Lilith in Sagittarius: founder of scientology L Ron Hubbard, founder of depth psychology Carl Jung, founder of theosophy Madame Blavatsky, a founder of the United States Thomas Jefferson and the Beast himself, Aleister Crowley. That is an extraordinary list of individuals to bring under one umbrella, but they are bound by the breadth of their unfettered thinking, and their ability to inspire others. Blavatsky, Crowley and Jung also exemplified a Sagittarian trait, taking inspiration themselves from multiple cultural sources. All were also prolific communicators — writing, arguing, lecturing and teaching. What's also notable is that Blavatsky, Hubbard and Crowley all founded cults, and Jung, although it may not have been his plan, spawned a following that is like a religion complete with holy texts and apostles.

So, if you were in the mood to start a cult and you happen to have Lilith in Sagittarius, perhaps it's a good career choice, but there are other avenues to explore, of course.

Another aspect of Lilith in Sagittarius exemplified by those thinkers is the visionary. American civil rights leader Martin Luther King has the placement, although his *Via Lamia* spills into the first degree of Capricorn, a sign of practical leadership. It's notable that American presidential contender Kamala Harris has the same configuration in the opposite direction: her Mean Lilith is in Capricorn and her *Via Lamia* moves back into visionary Sagittarius.

It occurred to me as I was writing this that the British marathon runner Paula Radcliffe looked like a Lilith in Sagittarius type, since this is also a sign of athleticism and long-distances. She does indeed have this placement. In contrast, Usain Bolt, the fastest short-distance runner in history, has Lilith in the opposite sign of that short distance, Gemini.

Many of my clients were born with Lilith in Sagittarius. As far as I am aware, none has started a religion yet, but nearly all of them have spent

Fictional heroine

Katniss Everdene is one of the great fictional heroines this century — freedom fighter, hunter, archer, revolutionary, athlete, truth-teller. She is bold, brave and kind. In the film of *The Hunger Games,* she is portrayed by Jennifer Lawrence, who will forever be identified with this role. Lawrence was born with Lilith rising in Sagittarius, the sign of the archer, and the role exemplifies all the best attributes of Lilith in Sagittarius. Here is a person at home in the wild: free thinking, adaptable, intelligent, curious, brave.

part of their adult lives living abroad. They have become strangers in a strange land — and for the most part this has set them free and allowed them to thrive. One client springs to mind in particular, who not only moved abroad as a young adult but now works on global issues, always taking the helicopter view. Another is a creator of worlds, a writer; and another is a life-long student of the occult.

All these are Sagittarian interests, and other parts of their charts do not quite show how these areas are important to them. These are areas of liberation, where the mind, or body, can freewheel, free-associate and soar. I think this appears to be a lucky placement in some ways, perhaps because truly, Lilith loves the wild places of Sagittarius.

A Powerful Lilith Return

In the mid-teens of this century, the #MeToo movement took off when the actress Alyssa Milano tweeted the following: "If you've been sexually harassed or assaulted write 'me too' as a reply to this tweet." This was in the wake of the Harvey Weinstein scandal in which one of Hollywood's most powerful producers stood accused of multiple charges of rape and sexual assault. The response to Milano's tweet, inspired by activist Tarana Burke, snowballed into a mass sharing of the experience of sexual harassment, revealing just how pervasive it is.

Alyssa Milano has a pretty good relationship with her own Lilith at 3° Sagittarius, which is in conjunction with glamorous Neptune, the planet associated with the silver screen, and the planet of conversation, Mercury in her chart. Appropriately, she will be forever remembered as Phoebe Halliwell, witch and demon-lover from the TV series *Charmed* that aired in the early noughties.

On 15 October 2017, when Milano posted her famous Me Too tweet, turbo-charging the #MeToo movement, Lilith, by transit, was exactly on Milano's Sun at 27° Sagittarius, the sign of publishing and mass communication. This is a once every nine years transit.

Some famous people with Lilith in Sagittarius

Ed Sheeran, Martin Luther King, Patti Smith, Marina Abramović, Gianni Versace, Elfriede Jelinek, Napoleon Bonaparte, Serena Williams, Pharrell Williams, Aleister Crowley, Alyssa Milano, Madame Blavatsky, Paula Radcliffe, Donald Trump, Bill Gates, Jennifer Lawrence, Audrey Hepburn, Carl Jung, Keanu Reeves, David Bowie

Best: brave adventurer

Worst: unbridled

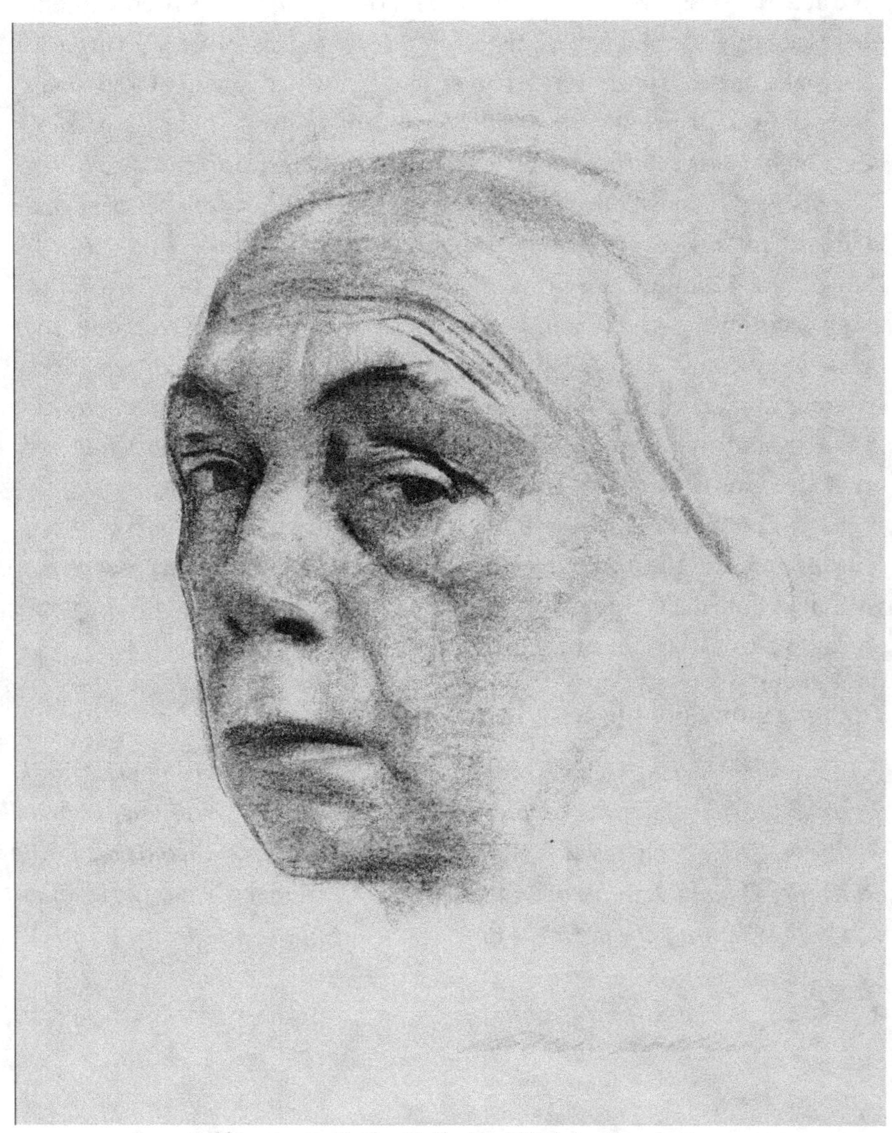

Self portrait. Kathe Kollwitz. Lilith in Capricorn

Capricorn

"There is a pleasure in the pathless woods,
There is a rapture on the lonely shore,
There is society, where none intrudes,
By the deep sea, and music in its roar:
I love not man the less, but Nature more"

— Lord Byron, 'Childe Harold's Pilgrimage'

"there is a loneliness in this world so great that you can see it in the slow movement of the hands of a clock."

— Charles Bukowski, 'Oh, look at the time'

"Think for yourself. Question authority."

— Timothy Leary

"Monsters are real, and ghosts are real too. They live inside us, and sometimes, they win."

— Stephen King

"The secret of life, though, is to fall seven times and to get up eight times."

— Paulo Coelho, *The Alchemist*

"In the end, a simple happiness is better than a complex disillusion."

— Janelle Monáe

"Who controls the past controls the future. Who controls the present controls the past."

— George Orwell, *1984*

Lilith in Capricorn

5 November 1902–31 July 1903
11 September 1911–5 June 1912
19 July 1920–10 April 1921
22 May 1929–14 February 1930
27 March 1938–22 December 1938
30 January 1947–27 October 1947
6 December 1955–31 August 1956
10 October 1964–7 July 1965
15 August 1973–12 May 1974
20 June 1982–18 March 1983
25 April 1991–21 January 1992
29 February 2000–25 November 2000
3 January 2009–1 October 2009
9 November 2017–6 August 2018
14 September 2026–11 June 2027
21 July 2035–15 April 2036

> "It is difficult to find happiness within oneself, but it is impossible to find it anywhere else."
>
> — Arthur Schopenhauer

> "People should either be caressed or crushed. If you do them minor damage they will get their revenge; but if you cripple them there is nothing they can do. If you need to injure someone, do it in such a way that you do not have to fear their vengeance."
>
> — Niccolo Machiavelli

> "It's a curious idea to reproduce when you don't even like life."
>
> — Michel Houellebecq

> "Can I tell you something about apricots? ... 1 in 30 is a good one. It's such a low percentage fruit."
>
> — Larry David

If you have Lilith in Capricorn, you may find your relationship with authority is very important to you. This authority may be a parent initially, and later it may be a boss, the work or the government itself.

You may find yourself either rebelling actively against the 'man', or inadvertently in hot water. If this is a pattern in your life, it's worth looking at transits to your natal Lilith. It's important to figure out your relationship with authority that is outside yourself, and your own inner sense of authority which may be unruly, exaggerated or missing.

It's interesting to imagine Lilith here, on Capricorn's mountain, surveying the world. And indeed, on a quite simple astrological level, you may find that you have an abiding passion for mountains and high places, old cities or ancient ruins.

On a different note, you may also find you have an exaggerated attitude to work itself or an exaggerated ambition. For example, you may have a job that forces you to work all the time, be the kind of person who is busy sending dozens of texts while you should be having dinner with the family, or you may somehow manage to avoid a 'real' job and be able to create or manage yourself into something that suits you.

I have clients at either end of this spectrum with Lilith in Capricorn. Some of them are extremely ambitious workaholics, and some somehow never quite manage to fit into society enough to have that standard issue job. Several have found themselves working for quite dark institutions by accident. I have one client who found herself caught up in the Enron scandal, for example. Interestingly, she ended up as an advocate for sustainable farming: farming is also a Capricorn interest.

But back to authority. Perhaps one of the most important books of the 20th century, *1984*, was written by George Orwell, born with Lilith in Capricorn, during his Lilith Return in 1947. It's a book that deals with a dystopian future when a totalitarian state has taken over that monitors your very thoughts. It's the origin of the concept of 'Big Brother' watching you, the 'thought police' and 'newspeak'. Orwell describes a total authority gone utterly mad, digging into its citizens' brains.

Carrie

American writer Stephen King's first novel *Carrie* burst into the world on 5 April 1975, introducing the reading public to a teenage girl with special powers of telekinesis. Carrie, the eponymous heroine, is archetypal Lilith. She is despised and cast out by her peers, and humiliated for having her period, which connects her to the lunar cycle.

The book culminates in a scene of gory mayhem, which was fabulously recreated in the film a couple of years after the book's publication with Lilith/Carrie taking her revenge on her tormentors. Interestingly, part of this climax is a kind of inverse coronation as prom queen, when Carrie has a bucket of pig's blood tipped over her head.

King's own Lilith is in hard-working Capricorn at 25°. On the day of publication, Lilith, by transit, was back at 25° Capricorn. Perhaps she has been his muse ever since.

The political strategist, Niccolò Machiavelli, adviser to the Medicis of Renaissance Florence, also has the placement, and just as we know what Orwellian means — a type of totalitarian mind invasion — we all know what Machiavellian means — a way of doing politics by manipulating people behind the scenes. Machiavelli's book *The Prince* is about how to wield power effectively. Both the authors have a sense of how an entire system of government could work. Government is a realm of Capricorn — both good and bad. This is a sign that's about vertical hierarchies and when

Lilith gets here, she can mess things up. It's notable that the grand-daddy of conspiracy theorists, talk radio host Alex Jones, has Lilith in Capricorn. It's a hyperfocused Lilith with almost no *Via Lamia*, and one might argue that he has been dedicated to bringing down successive American governments by spreading disinformation. During the years when Pluto, Lord of Power, travelled through Capricorn (2008-2024) Jones was particularly lethally active. Another challenger to the American system of government in recent years — from the other direction — was Edward Snowden, a security contractor who leaked information about how the US government kept people under surveillance. Indeed, Big Brother turned out to be watching you and me, and quite a lot of surprising people. Snowden was indicted for espionage and fled to Russia. This can be another theme of Lilith in Capricorn.

Lilith in Capricorn people may find themselves cast out of their own countries unwillingly sometimes, like Snowden, although quite a few may find themselves achieving a higher status abroad. A notable example is American movie star Grace Kelly, who was elevated to Princess Grace of Monaco. It's also notable that quite a few Lilith in Capricorn people on my books have married a powerful or famous person, becoming a regal spouse like Kelly.

US politician Hillary Clinton has Lilith in Capricorn and she exemplifies several aspects of this placement. She rose to power through her marriage, but was vilified as a kind of witch. Mind you, her tenacity is likely more to do with her Scorpio placements. When she made her own run for presidency, all the old Lilith stereotypes came into play. She has an awkward relationship with authority. Although she possesses much, and has been at the table of power, she is always cast out or cast in the role of witch when she is there.

It's an interesting dichotomy. This is both a powerful placement for anyone ambitious, and a tricky one.

Some famous people with Lilith in Capricorn

Grace Kelly, Aishwarya Rai, Penelope Cruz, Bryan Cranston, Elisabeth Moss, Machiavelli, Mata Hari, Edward Snowden, Alex Jones, Edward VIII, Lord Byron, Chris Rock, Kate Moss, Stephen King, Marie Curie, Anthony Bourdain, Charles Bukowski, Anais Nin, Paulo Coelho

Best: queen of the underworld
Worst: king of the gutter

Aquarius

"You were once wild here. Don't let them tame you."

— Isadora Duncan

"Without self knowledge, without understanding the working and functions of his machine, man cannot be free, he cannot govern himself and he will always remain a slave."

— G.I. Gurdjieff

"When we deny the EVIL within ourselves, we dehumanise ourselves, and we deprive ourselves not only of our own destiny but of any possibility of dealing with the EVIL of others."

— J. Robert Oppenheimer

"We must be willing to let go of the life we planned so as to have the life that is waiting for us."

— Joseph Campbell

"It is no measure of health to be well adjusted to a profoundly sick society."

— J. Krishnamurti

"Those who can imagine anything, can create the impossible."

— Alan Turing

"Yet if a woman never lets herself go, how will she ever know how far she might have got? If she never takes off her high-heeled shoes, how will she ever know how far she could walk or how fast she could run?"

— Germaine Greer

I'm sane, but I'm overwhelmed
I'm lost, but I'm hopeful...

— Alanis Morissette, 'Hands in My Pocket'

"Emptiness comes as sunset comes of an evening, full of beauty, enchantment and richness; it comes as naturally as the blossoming of a flower. "

— Jiddu Krishnamurti

Self portrait. Jo Koster. Lilith in Aquarius

So wild Lilith arrives in Aquarius, the sign of fixed air, where systems of ideas are codified and organised. This is a place of science and community, solitude and free thinking.

If you have this placement, you may struggle with a desire to be accepted and a yearning to break utterly free from society's strictures. There are many radical thinkers with this placement, but looking through my files I find also that there are several people in my books who have risen high up in government and other really big systems of endeavour. The question is: are you going to be inside the tent, or outside? Either way it's likely that your relationship with certain sets of ideas — a religion, a science, politics, the patriarchy — will be a source of freedom or repression, irritation or inspiration.

The feminist Germaine Greer is an example of someone who did both. She worked from within the great institutions of academia to critique society. So although she criticised the patriarchy, she was also part of the power structure. The same is true of many race and gender critical theorists, of course, and the point may be that they are choosing to make change from within.

Aquarius is a sign of engineering, big electrical grids, big human networks like the internet itself. This may be where your Lilith operates.

But there is another side to Aquarius too. This is the sign of the mountain-top, the hermit, but also the sign of those wind-swept city streets. The weirdos at the edge of the world — and even beyond this planet. Aquarius is a sign of alienation and aliens themselves. The dilemma for Aquarius is often how to balance the desire to rebel and be individual with a need to be part of a group or contribute to society. This tension can be exacerbated by Lilith. Are you in with the in crowd? Or are you more comfortable on the edge of the village eating nettle soup? You may find that you have to bounce back and forth between those two places.

As a Lilith in Aquarius person, you may feel comfortable on the wild edge of things. Germaine Greer, in later life, split her time between a patch of rainforest that she bought in Australia and the stony halls of Cambridge University.

The author JK Rowling, creator of Harry Potter, has Lilith in Aquarius, and indeed her writings exemplify some of the associations of this placement. Her Lilith is exactly opposite to her extraordinarily creative Leo Sun. These are both fixed signs,

Lilith in Aquarius

31 July 1903–25 April 1904
5 June 1912–28 February 1913
10 April 1921–4 January 1922
14 February 1930–9 November 1930
21 December 1938–15 September 1939
27 October 1947–21 July 1948
31 August 1956–26 May 1957
7 July 1965–1 April 1966
12 May 1974–5 February 1975
15 August 1973–12 May 1974
18 March 1983–12 December 1983
21 January 1992–17 October 1992
25 November 2000–22 August 2001
1 October 2009–28 June 2010
6 August 2018–3 May 2019
11 June 2027–8 March 2028
15 April 2036–11 January 2037

Selling Sex

Lilith is feared as a seducer of men, a woman on the edge of society, not following the rules, which sounds a bit like a prostitute, or the woman at the edge of the village who is a sex worker.

Back in the 1990s, Heidi Fleiss was exposed as the Madame of an upscale prostitution ring in Hollywood, with allegedly many A-list clients. It was all over the papers for ages as she went through various trials, got convicted and sold her story.

Fleiss has a conjunction of Lilith and Venus in Aquarius in the first house. Venus is, of course, the planet associated with pleasure but also with money, and the delta of Venus itself. Aquarius is the sign of social networks — apparently Fleiss's address book was quite special. Interestingly, American porn star Stormy Daniels, who took Donald Trump to court, also has Lilith and Venus interacting in her chart. They are opposed across Aquarius-Leo, the common person vs the king. There is Stormy, comfortable with her 'shocking' career, regarding the king himself.

orderly signs. Her Lilith is reflecting her Leo Sun. Rowling created a plausible world which is within ours and parallel to it, where magic is possible. The wizarding world is still bound by very specific rules, and social mores. It's not so different from our world: men still seem to run the show, and many women are figures of fun or insanity, as in the case of Bellatrix Lestrange, who is an avatar of Lilith for sure.

A scrambled mind may be a feature of Lilith in Aquarius, for example you may have an addiction to conspiracy theories, a need to think outside the box that takes your mind into the woods. But another way this could work is through a love of giant systems of ideas — for example astrology or computer science. For example, Alan Turing, born with Lilith in Aquarius, whose work during World War II started the computing age, was incontestably a brilliant mathematician, and his work travelled to the very edges of human thought. The Turing test is still used today to decide if AI can actually pass for human. In his own life, Turing also encountered Lilith energy at its most terrible. The British government in the 1940s forced chemical castration on Turing, because he was gay. This is a horrible punishment in any circumstances, but somehow more extraordinary to inflict on a person whose work may well have shortened WW2 by several years. In other words, Turing was

Bad Feminist

Roxane Gay, author of *Bad Feminist*, has a fascinating astrological chart by any standards, with a tight stellium in the sign of justice, Libra, that trines her Lilith in alienated Aquarius.

Many feminists have Lilith in an air sign — Libra, Aquarius, Gemini. These are the signs of the intellectual, and Lilith in any of these signs can bring radical ideas, an ability to think outside the box, or, as our corporate friends would have it, blue-sky thinking.

a mathematical war hero, but society punished him brutally for his sexual preferences. In the end, he killed himself.

Turing was a numbers genius, of course, and we very much associate numbers with the sign Aquarius. It's a sign that sees patterns. So it's noteworthy that two of the most successful investors of the 20th and 21st century, George Soros and Warren Buffett, have this placement. There are other elements in their charts which explain their great wealth, but the ability to see through a spreadsheet and be extraordinarily playful with numbers may have something to do with Lilith in Aquarius. Both have also been serious philanthropists. This is quite interesting since Aquarius is the sign of the common person — as opposed to the sign of kings, Leo.

Some famous people with Lilith in Aquarius

Geena Davis, Jackson Pollack, Amy Winehouse, Mila Kunis, JK Rowling, Alan Turing, Germaine Greer, Bjork, Shahrukh Khan, Salman Khan, Warren Buffett, Cindy Crawford, Ludwig van Beethoven, Edgar Cayce, Adam Driver, Mads Mikkelsen, Daniel Day-Lewis, Cary Grant, Amy Adams, Charli XCX, Rachida Dati, Neil Armstrong, Rosa Parks, George Soros, Jennette McCurdy, Nathalie Baye, Dane Rudhyar, Kajol, Hermann Hesse, Francis Ford Coppola, Bradley Cooper, JK Rowling, Alanis Morissette

Best: relentless humanitarian

Worst: amoral

Pisces

"The universe is an example of love. Like a tree. Like the ocean. Like my body. Like my wheelchair. I see the love."

— Ram Dass

"Sometimes when I look at you, I feel I'm gazing at a distant star. It's dazzling, but the light is from tens of thousands of years ago. Maybe the star doesn't even exist any more. Yet sometimes that light seems more real to me than anything."

— Haruki Murakami, *South of the Border, West of the Sun*

"Perhaps man has a hundred senses, and when he dies only the five senses that we know perish with him, and the other ninety-five remain alive."

— Anton Chekhov, *The Cherry Orchard*

"If all the world hated you and believed you wicked, while your own conscience approved of you and absolved you from guilt, you would not be without friends."

— Charlotte Brontë

"Telle est la vie des hommes. Quelques joies, très vite effacées par d'inoubliables chagrins."

— Marcel Pagnol

It's about soul in Pisces — a beautiful soul, a large, multifarious soul or a soul that has been somehow burnt to a crisp. As with all astrology, there is a polarity to Pisces. An extreme Piscean may be rolling in the gutter or twinkling among the stars.

Here is the sign of unbounded imagination, music, spirituality. Innumerable soulful, and not so soulful singers have Lilith in Pisces, because as we know, she can bestow prodigious talents. To name a few 21st century stars: Ariana Grande, Billie Eilish, Harry Styles and Miley Cyrus, were all born with Lilith in the sign of the fishes. And interestingly they were all groomed to stardom from childhood. One of the most famous child stars of them all, Judy Garland, also has this placement. There are many other factors in all their charts, of course, but it's noteworthy that

Self-portrait sketch. Albrecht Durer. Lilith in Pisces

they share a certain malleability as well as musical talent. Pisces is the most flowing sign of all, since it is 'mutable water'. There are many more great singers in particular who have this placement: for example, Marvin Gaye, Donna Summer, Tom Jones, Stevie Nicks and Robert Plant from an older generation.

Lilith in Pisces

25 April 1904–21 Jan 1905
28 February 1913–26 November 1913
4 January 1922–1 October 1922
9 November 1930–6 August 1931
15 September 1939–11 June 1940
21 July 1948–16 April 1949
26 May 1957–19 February 1958
1 April 1966–26 December 1966
5 Feb 1975–31 October 1975
12 December 1983–5 September 1984
17 October 1992–14 July 1993
22 August 2001–17 May 2002
28 June 2010–23 March 2011
3 May 2019–27 January 2020
8 March 2028–2 December 2028
11 January 2037–7 October 2037

One of the most tragic rock and roll deaths of the late 20th century was the drowning of the singer Jeff Buckley, who floated away one night in the Mississippi. He had barely crossed the threshold of fame, as his extraordinary first album had just been released. He had the voice of an angel, and sang of otherworldly love and otherworldly places. His rendition of Leonard Cohen's 'Hallelluljah' turned that song into an anthem of pain and longing. His Lilith is in watery Pisces, in the eighth house of death, making an exact trine aspect to his Sun in deepest Scorpio, also a water sign.

That connection to the mystery, the unseen or the numinous can be a powerful factor for people with Lilith in Pisces. 20th century spiritual pioneers, Rudolf Steiner, Ram Dass, and Joseph Campbell were all Lilith in Pisces. But there is also a dark side to this placement. The notorious cult leader Jim Jones, who led his followers to a mass suicide in the jungles of Guyana in the late 1970s, had Lilith in Pisces. So did Osama Bin Laden, one of the theological thinkers behind the 9/11 attack on the World Trade Center.

As you may know Pisces also rules the feet. One example is the English footballer David Beckham who was said to be able to bend the trajectory of a ball, a magician with his feet. He has Mars (sports) in Pisces conjoined by Lilith. Cristiano Ronaldo, often voted the greatest footballer of them all, has Mean Lilith in Aries, but his *Via Lamia* runs across Pisces and fiery Aries.

Musical Prodigy

During his lifetime, Gustav Mahler was one of the most successful conductors of the Hapsburg empire, partly due to his sheer genius, which showed itself from a very early age. He was born with the Moon rising, chased by a powerful Lilith and Neptune, all in the musical sign of Pisces. Lilith also makes a close trine to Mahler's highly sensitive Cancer Sun.

Since his death, he has been hailed as one of the greatest composers in the western canon. He is considered the last of the romantic composers, perfect for a person with the Moon on the ascendant. Original, experimental, open to many musical influences, and deeply knowledgeable.

In his lifetime, he was noted for his numerous, hectic love affairs, as you might expect with Lilith and the Moon in the ascendant. He was also a temperamental boss, by most accounts, highly sociable and extremely diligent and focused on music. Although he had converted to Catholicism he was often targeted by the yellow press for his Jewishness. There is the Lilith theme of being a lifelong outsider, even though he moved easily through the *haute bourgeois* salons of late 19th and early 20th century central Europe, where Jews and non-Jews mingled.

He married the much younger composer, Alma, on 2 March 1902 with a New Moon on his natal Lilith. The marriage was famously rocky as he tried to stop Alma creating music and she went off having affairs, putting him in the unfamiliar role of cuckold. She outlived him by 50 years and managed his legacy, and after a few decades, like Frida Kahlo (Lilith in Cancer) Mahler's reputation began to grow even greater after death than before.

Reputational Abyss

The extraordinary contrast between two recipients of the Nobel prize for literature illustrates some of the power of Lilith in this sign of the imagination.

The Nobel-prize winning Canadian writer Alice Munro may, in the future, be remembered less for her brilliant, finely-cut stories than for her failure to protect her own daughter from the sexual predations of her husband.

As Neptune, a planet that brings both scandal and cleansing, sailed across Munro's Lilith in Pisces, her daughter revealed that not only had her step-father repeatedly assaulted her as a child, but her mother, when she found out, had responded as if she were the injured party. It's impossible to read a story by Alice Munro again without that awareness of her own, flawed nature.

This story is in itself, in the realm of Lilith, of course, There is the abandoned child, and in the mind of Munro apparently, also the three-way relationship. Pisces is the sign of no-boundaries, also sometimes no rules, and also the victim. The husband molests the nine-year-old child; the wife responds to this news as if he had taken an adult lover, and she were the victim.

What makes this story more strange is the fact that Munro was especially lauded for her psychological insight, her perception, her understanding of the human condition. Yet when it came to someone truly close to her, her own child, she utterly failed. Pisces is also the sign of victimhood, and it seems Munro chose to occupy that space only for herself and her fictional characters.

This perceptiveness is undoubtedly marked in the chart by her Pluto-Sun conjunction, however that also may have created the black hole in her vision. The conjunction is in the sign of motherhood, Cancer.

Munro's Piscean Lilith is part of a tight watery configuration. Lilith, in her first house, makes a perfect trine aspect to her lucky Jupiter, exalted in Cancer and in the house of work. Not only was her private life filled with Lilith themes, so was the work she produced. Both then make perfect aspects to her midheaven, the place of reputation, which was both exalted (Jupiter) and then brought down to the gutter (Lilith).

The Stranger

Albert Camus, the highly influential French author and philosopher, most famous for *The Plague* and *The Stranger* was born with the writer's sign, Virgo, rising. In the opposite house, in boundless Pisces, sits Lilith, staring straight into his eyes. That particular position of Lilith is interestingly frequent for writers.

The main themes of his work? Alienation, irrationality, meaninglessness…

Reputational Glory

In contrast, Nobel-prize-winning writer Toni Morrison's reputation has grown exponentially since her death. She has an extraordinarily powerfully placed Black Moon Lilith, which makes an exact conjunction to her own Pisces Moon.

Her work frequently deals with Lilith themes — dead babies, abuse, being outcast, harmful mothers, the strength in being an outsider, the power of acknowledging the hard truths: slavery, brutality, murder.

If you want a masterclass in what Lilith means from one of the richest and most complex imaginations of modern times, read her novel *Beloved*, in which she defines the greatness of Lilith, especially in the complexity of mother-child relationships in a cruel world. Everything is there. Read no further in this section, if you want to avoid spoilers.

Beloved herself is a ghost, or possibly not a ghost, of a child murdered by her own mother, Sethe, who killed her rather than allowing her to be taken back into slavery. Sethe is a mother forced to make an impossible choice, who is then haunted for the rest of her life. This is a situation that is so close to the apocryphal Lilith, the ancient demoness cast out by Adam.

One of the central characters, Baby Suggs seems also to be an embodiment of Lilith in Pisces, the sign of priests. Baby Suggs was born into slavery. She had nine children, eight of whom were taken from her, and sold, just as Lilith loses 100 babies a day. But her freedom is bought for her by her son, Halle, who is eventually driven mad himself by the horrors inflicted on his pregnant wife. When Baby Suggs finally reaches Cincinnati, Ohio, she becomes a preacher and healer. "When warm weather came, Baby Suggs, holy, followed by every black man, woman, and child who could make it through, took her great heart to the Clearing… Finally she called the women to her. 'Cry,' she told them. 'For the living and the dead. Just cry." And that is one of the powers of Lilith in Pisces, the ability and willingness to grieve whole-heartedly, and to act as an emotional conduit for others to grieve and heal.

It's an extraordinarily powerful book — and despite the terrifying subject matter, full of vigour and humanity, full of the creative, resilient power of Lilith.

Some famous people with Lilith in Pisces

Toni Morrison, Alice Munro, Judy Garland, Michel de Montaigne, Niki Lauda, Gustav Mahler, Johannes Brahms, Jeff Buckley, Tina Turner, Salvador Dali, Jack White, Samuel L Jackson, Eric Cantona, Cat Stevens, Carlos Slim Helú, Mark Zuckerberg, Halle Berry.

Best: artistic genius
Worst: endless victim

Chapter Four

Houses & Angles

Locating Lilith within the natal chart will tell you where to look for her in your life. Each house of the chart represents thematic areas of your existence, for example, the second house represents our resources, income and expenditure; the fourth house, our roots. At the start of each section, there's a précis of the themes of that house, but do use your imagination to extrapolate. For example, the third house may hold our schooling, neighbours and siblings, but it also tells us about our minds, our skill, or lack thereof, in language and communications — and you may be able to see from this list that it is also where we look at short journeys, commuting and cars.

Lilith themes to look for are exile, outrageous talent, allure, humour, cruelty, abuse, prolificness, excess, rule-breaking, wildness, nature-loving, animal-loving, thresholds of birth and death, and sex.

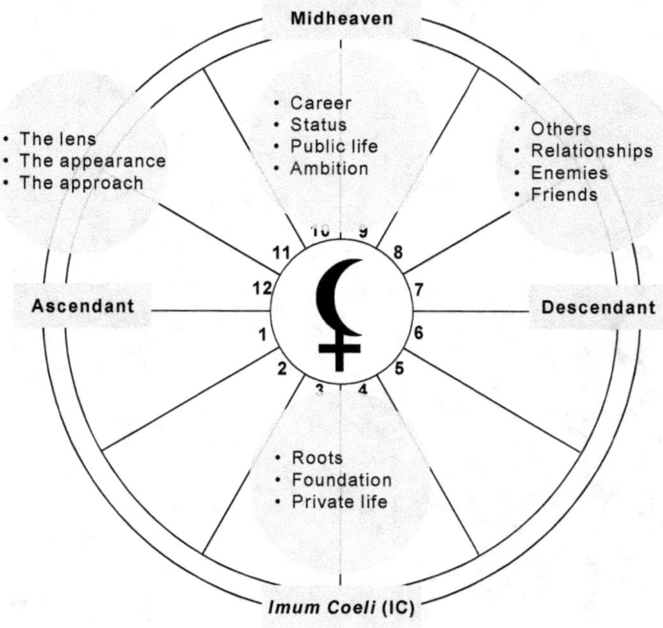

You may well find the house in which your Lilith falls is far more potent than the sign. This is because it's actually more personal to you; the house cusps change from one minute to the next, moving like a clock through the 360-degree circle.

At the time you were born, a particular constellation will have been coming over the horizon. This is called the 'Ascendant' or 'rising sign'. So you may have Cancer or Scorpio or Libra rising, for example. This rising sign begins the so-called 'first house' of your horoscope. From that first house hang eleven more in a circle, dividing the horoscope or birth chart into 12 slices of pie. The houses tell you where in your life events may take place.

Any planet or point close to one of the four angles of a chart, the cusps of the first, tenth, seventh and fourth houses, known as the Ascendant, Midheaven, Descendant and the *Imum Coeli* (IC) — is immediately empowered, and may have a pivotal effect on life and character.

So the house placement of Lilith tells you where she may be most often at work, and the sign placement tells you how. This Lilith by sign and house is your personal Lilith who will stay with you through your life, evolving, emerging and submerging, as you go through the world. Sometimes she will be strong, and sometimes silent, but she is always there.

The Voice of a Poet

The American nature poet Mary Oliver has an extraordinarily powerfully placed Lilith. It's directly on her Ascendant and in the heart of her Sun. She both embodied Lilith in some sense, saw the world through the eyes of Lilith, and spoke the truth of Lilith. Much of her poetry centres around her intense engagement with the natural world.

As a Virgo, Oliver was also deeply attentive to the craft of poetry, and to her own sensual responses. This is given enormous vigour by Lilith.

Many of her poems are familiar to you, perhaps, but the line that is most often quoted from her oeuvre is this one from 'The Summer Day'.

> *Tell me, what is it you plan to do with your one wild and precious life?*

Imagine that this is Lilith herself speaking.

If you're interested in exploring your chart more deeply as you go through this book, there are plenty of websites where you can get it drawn up for free. Make sure you are looking at the 'Mean' Lilith rather than the 'True'. This will likely be under 'calculations'. And look for the symbol to see which house your Lilith lives in. After you have fully absorbed the meaning of her house and sign, look at the True Lilith also, and you will see your *Via Lamia,* which may well stay within one house and sign anyway.

First House

The face, your outlook, the impression you make on others, the lens through which you initially see the world.

Look for your Lilith in the mirror and in the eyes of other people when they look at you.

With Lilith in the first house, you may well be seen as an outsider, or find yourself on the outside. This may simply be because of the circumstances you were born into, or because something happened later in life to make you an outsider. When Lilith is here she may be speaking through you, displaying some aspect of herself through you, and you may use Lilith as your mask. For example, the Femme Fatale quality of Lilith is often an easy mask for some women with this placement to don.

I've come across quite a few people with this signature who have moved to a foreign country as adults. It's actually worked out well, as they feel comfortable in the position of recognised alien. Indeed, living in a strange land suits them better than being surrounded by the people they grew up with. This outsider identity may be something that's quite easy for others to see or hear — for example, you may speak with an accent.

Outsiderishness has its advantages. Lilith in the first can make you hard to 'place', compartmentalise or classify, and in the same way can set you free of certain social inhibitions, which helps you to see more truthfully. It also means that people who like to classify other people, for example snobs, have trouble figuring you out. This can make you socially mobile — up or down — and less attached to the usual mores.

First house Lilith is also a signature — sometimes — of the long-term mistress or cuckold. In some way, you may see yourself as 'spare' in love relationships, the bit on the side, or the person who gets cheated on. I've had several clients with this placement who were serially mistresses for many years, but all found themselves eventually married — somewhat to their surprise. The triangular relationship is a Lilith theme; after all she was Adam's first wife. One woman I know married her long-term lover after finally getting him away from his wife only to find she was very bored. They were divorced within a couple of years.

First house Lilith can also bring a lot of sexual allure. This may not even be obvious 'sexiness', but just something about you that speaks to other's desires. On the flip side, Lilith in the first may also bring a relentless sex-drive; the famously virile artist Pablo Picasso had this placement.

Lilith Rising

Most superstars of the 1950s are no longer household names, but Marilyn Monroe is still recognised by every generation, even 60 years after her death. She was born with Lilith rising; that is Lilith precisely on her Ascendant, so Lilith is exactly what we see when we look at her, and she is also channeling aspects of Lilith outwards. With Lilith so exactly on an angle like this, you might expect the Black Moon to dominate Monroe's life and indeed her biography reads like a whole series of Lilith tales. From a childhood of abuse to her multiple miscarriages to her tremendous charisma, Monroe embodied Lilith energy.

Monroe is known to millions from the silver screen, and even her simple image, the picture of her beautiful face. We have a one-to-one experience of her. From this Ascendant, Monroe is expressing aspects of Lilith —from victim to sex bomb to free spirit. One of the songs she sings in the film *Some Like It Hot* is 'Running Wild' — and that is certainly part of her appeal. She's beautiful, a film star — and yet somehow available. In many of her roles, she plays a woman on the edge of crazy. Most of her best roles are in comedies, which is an important aspect of Lilith: remember how the she-demon tickles babies' feet. Another aspect of Monroe's enormous appeal was her apparent mixture of innocence and sexuality; her baby face and childish voice. Monroe's Lilith was in Leo, the actor's sign. Monroe would talk about putting on 'Marilyn' like a mask before meeting the press.

Her Aquarian Moon — often a placement that brings the common touch, an ability to be at one with the people, popularity — is directly opposite her Lilith, in the house of the 'other', of you, as opposed to me.

Clearly, Lilith on the Ascendant has its dangers. American novelist Norman Mailer expressed a particular response to Lilith on the Ascendant when he said of Monroe: "She is a mirror of the pleasure of those who stare at her." Of course, Monroe was much more than that — a fully formed person, not just mirror.

Her personal life was also a series of Lilith stories. On one hand, she was horribly abused as a child, and a victim of the casting couch. Monroe did not know who her father was, and her mother was a damaged, unstable woman, which meant that she was fostered by many different families. She grew up an outsider. As an adult, Monroe was married several times, never able to settle down as a 'wife', and she also suffered multiple miscarriages.

On the other hand, she remade herself by getting educated: hanging out with smart people, reading profound books, taking classes at the Actor's Studio, marrying one of America's biggest intellectuals of the 1950s. And by becoming 'Marilyn', the biggest star in Hollywood, with all the clout that glamour brings, she made herself powerful.

That also is a Lilith story — the tale of a person treated like trash by society who eventually triumphs.

Monroe was also an activist — although the word was not really used at the time. She was against nuclear armament, in favour of civil rights. She famously stood up for the great jazz singer Ella Fitzgerald when the latter was having trouble getting gigs because of the colour of her skin.

Ella Fitzgerald (left) and Marilyn Monroe (right) both born with Lilith Rising. Can you see her in the look?

Fascinatingly, Fitzgerald also has Lilith directly on her Ascendant in the same sign as Monroe's, Leo. This signature is identical in both women's charts. Fitzgerald was nine years older than Monroe, born on a previous Lilith in Leo cycle.

Monroe used her star power, sitting in the front row with her famous friends, at Fitzgerald's shows. Fitzgerald later explained that she owed a great debt to Monroe.

The two women actually had similarly ropey childhoods, with lost parents. The orphaned Fitzgerald was eventually sent to a segregated correctional institution when she was a kid, and according to some sources was essentially tortured by male staff.

In some ways they responded similarly to these harsh starts. Fitzgerald became one of the greatest jazz singers of the 20th century, beloved by millions, and Monroe became the greatest sex symbol of her time, beloved by millions.

Fitzgerald's race made her an outsider in white America, even though her music was admired by everyone. Even at her own concerts in the 1950s, as a black woman she would literally have to come in the side entrance. She toured the country, entertaining the most privileged, yet unable to stay in the hotels or go to restaurants herself because of segregation laws.

So it's fascinating that her friendship with Monroe was a huge help in breaking through race laws.

Fitzgerald also had Monroe's uncanny allure — but it was not her face, but her voice where the star power showed. She has a conjunction of Venus, the planet of beauty, and the Sun, in Taurus, the sign of the throat on the Midheaven of her chart.

Both these stars have an eternal quality to their work, which seems to cut through time, even though they were both huge in their own time.

Second House

Money, values, self-valuation, security, income and expenditure, how we earn a living, talents, what we have that others want, material needs and desires.

Find your own Lilith in your attitudes to money, values or possessions.

Well, Lilith in your second house does not indicate poverty. Beyoncé Knowles has this placement in Scorpio, and so does Rishi Sunak, the richest man ever to be prime minister of Britain. In fact, one thing these two have in common is conspicuous consumption. Perhaps their material needs are without boundaries. In my own files, I note an exceptionally talented accountant with this placement.

With Lilith here, you may have an outstanding or unusual talent that some people envy and others find fascinating. Often where Lilith falls in our chart is the place we are willing to go the extra mile, be outside the norm, leave the pack behind. In the second house, this could be to do with how you earn a living, of course, or your system of values.

Philip Pullman, author of the *His Dark Materials* trilogy, has Lilith conjoining his South Node in Sagittarius, in this part of his natal chart. Pullman has a remarkably rich imagination, and it's probably true to say that *His Dark Materials*, which takes place both in our own world and in an alternative parallel world, is his masterpiece. It's also quite a literal expression of Lilith in the second: that is Dark=Lilith, Materials=second house.

A driving force of the trilogy — spoiler alert — is Pullman's philosophy. He is a fierce atheist. Sagittarius is the sign of organised religion, and the South Node can show what we are letting go of that also propels us forward like a turbo. It's possible that Lilith here is quietly sowing the seeds of anti-Church in her anarchic mode. The heroine of his story is actually called Lyra, an echo of the name Lilith, and it is her unwillingness to conform to her parents' wishes that initiates the action of the novels.

So Lilith here will show you something about a person's values — which may be unusual, or contrary, different or out of synch. Your beliefs may set you apart. Prince Harry grew up privileged in some ways and deprived in others. There was no shortage of money, but his second house Lilith in Aries has certainly played a part in his story. His values or beliefs are different from those of his family, and he's been willing to bust every taboo around the carefully constructed value system in which he was raised.

What happens in the second house tends to be ideas that you have worked out for yourself, not ones that you receive. Aries means he is willing to fight for those different values. Indeed, in some ways, Lilith is a recurring theme in his story, appearing first as his own orphaning at the age of 11. On the day of Diana's death, Lilith and the North Node were in conjunction — wiping away the mother — a couple of degrees short of Harry's Virgo Sun. Then Lilith arrived as Camilla Parker Bowles, his father's mistress, and finally, his marriage to Meghan Markle has effectively cast him out of the royal family, because his values no longer align with theirs.

Harry's Lilith makes a perfect smooth trine aspect to Meghan's north node — her fate — in the sign of royalty, Leo. And there is written a story of an ordinary person raised to royalty and yet outcast. It's curious. I don't think you could have predicted exactly how it would turn out, since his initial rebellion might have sufficed.

His Lilith also sits directly opposite to Meghan's extraordinarily powerful stellium of Saturn, Jupiter and the Moon in Libra, the sign of marriage and partnership. I expect that not only has she provided a new country for his Lilith to escape to, but a new set of beliefs. Her own Lilith is in the fifth house of acting and children, conjoined by the planet of catalyst, Uranus. She herself is an agent of change, both through acting and the bearing of children.

So when we talk about the second house we often focus overly on the making and getting of money, whereas it's more useful to think of it as a place where we display and apply our values, our talent, or our sense of our own worth.

Nevertheless it is always important with Lilith here to ask about our money story. Do we feel poor or lacking? What is our self-worth? And what are our boundaries when it comes to making money, or spending it? I have several people on my books with this placement who have at some point 'sold their souls to the devil', and have spent a long time buying it back!

Third House

Siblings, schooling, communications, ideas, skills, mind, speech, writing. Driving, short trips, cars, transport, running.

Your Lilith may be a brother, sister or close friend — or the way your mind works. Don't be afraid of having outrageous ideas.

The good news with this placement is that you may have an unending stream of ideas bubbling through your brain, a stream of words spilling from your pen, or some outrageous skills that you might deploy.

The bad news is that you may have a brother or sister who betrays you, difficulty with normal schooling, and ideas that no one else likes.

I have a handful of clients with Lilith in the third who come from complex or unconventional families with, say, much older and much younger half-siblings, or simply a huge extended tribe, when nieces need to be treated like daughters, and uncles turn out to be grandfathers. This can be enriching, in fact, adding to the variety and interest of family life. I also have a few who simply grew up with a very disruptive sibling and have had to escape. And two particular clients who both had disabled siblings that profoundly influenced their life directions.

A negative example of this placement is Boris Johnson, ex-British Prime Minister with a very special relationship to the truth. For him, Lilith is in Sagittarius, the sign of publishing. And before his entry into politics, he had a successful career as a prolific journalist. Although he was sacked for making things up by one newspaper, others enjoyed his unusual level of mendacity. But his shtick was exaggeration and negativity, not coming up with actual ideas. In fact, Lilith shows herself in his chart, as exactly what she is in the sky — a void. Johnson's idea vacuum meant that he latched on to the negative. Eventually, this proved his undoing. Interestingly, his fellow Brexiteer UK politician Nigel Farage also has Lilith in the third. This is a man truly blessed with the ability to speak fluently and convincingly on seemingly any subject — and again, dissemble with the blithe insouciance of a child pretending they did not steal a cookie from the cookie jar.

Both these men have produced quite complex families of their own. Johnson has sired numerous offspring from different partners, and Farage has had two families. But this is nothing in comparisons to entrepreneur and wielder of chain-saws Elon Musk, whose birth family displayed all the complexity and challenge of this placement. The fate of one of his step-sisters, who bore two children to Musk's father, is weird, even by the standards of a Lilith tale. Musk has on the latest count had 13 children by various different women, and is presumably working on some more. There are other elements of his chart that contribute to this — but you can see that's Lilith's brood.

Elon Musk displays other positive and negative possibilities of Lilith in the third. He is a person bubbling with ideas that break rules or go out of bounds — for example his love of rockets. The electric car, Tesla, is a child of his fantasy, and his Lilith is in conjunction with the planet of invention, Uranus. Cars are a third house thing (transportation). Musk's Lilith is in Libra, the sign of the partners, and indeed all his ideas have come to life with the input of others. Mind you, he's not known for cleaving to the truth either, and don't forget siblings — step, half and full — are all found in the third. Musk is blessed with many. As I write this book, it is unclear what Musk's eventual fate will be — whether he will go down as a liar, end up on Mars or scramble his brains so badly with ketamine that he cannot continue. An unquiet mind is one of the dangers of this placement.

On the other hand (or foot), the great footballer Cristiano Ronaldo has the same placement — but it's in the sign of speed and initiative, Aries. Ronaldo is sometimes lauded as the greatest ever footballer. The third house can show us how we work with buddies or in a team, so he may be wildly inspiring for his footballing mates. Of course, Ronaldo's other stunningly successful effort has been as an influencer on social media, another third house area. For a while he had more followers on Instagram than anyone else on the planet.

With Lilith here, you may also have had trouble with normal schooling, because of your off-beat thinking or method of learning. Don't worry, you can find a place for yourself in the world. In fact, your unfettered ability to let your mind soar to the outer planets or plunge beneath the surface of the earth may turn out to be your talent.

Fourth House

Family, roots, origins, real estate, parents, home, foundations.

Lilith may have manifested as your mother or father, or in the birth family. Integrate her now by acknowledging her foundational presence in your development.

Lilith in the fourth house is a really interesting position. I've seen it in people who never really feel at home anywhere, but all have turned this to their advantage, by finding delight in being a stranger on whatever soil they find themselves putting down roots. Indeed, you might find that life takes you to a foreign land far away. There may be something essentially contested about the place you call home — or the family you come from.

You may also have an enduring love of wildness, or just feel more comfortable on a rugged heath, or in a blazing swamp, or on the wrong side of the tracks. Nature, or the earth itself, could be a great source of creative inspiration with this placement too. Walk barefoot, swim in wild places. The whole untamed planet is your home here.

Think of Lilith walking along the shoreline between the land and the sea, picking shells, feeling the sand between her toes and the salt water washing her thighs.

You may also feel some uncertainty about your parents. Are they really yours? Were you orphaned or adopted? Was your real dad the milkman?

It can be a sign of a disrupted childhood, or erratic parenting. A perfect example of this Lilith placement is the Hollywood actor Keanu Reeves. He was born in Beirut to an English mother and American father. His father abandoned the family when Reeves was three and he moved countries several times after that. The family eventually landed in Canada. He has Lilith in Sagittarius — the sign of exotic foreign parts — in the fourth.

Lilith on the IC

Lilith on the IC, the roots, the place of home and family can be quite disturbing. I have several clients with this placement who come from homes where sexual abuse was taking place.

It can also be a sign that the mother or significant carer did not take care or protect, or that either she or the native were cast out of the tribe in some manner. A strong Lilith can be a mark of insanity in the family, or of some important person who did not play by the rules or recognise society's rules. The late blues singer Billie Holiday, who came from an entirely broken home, had this signature, for example. It may also suggest illegitimacy. I have seen this in the charts of people who were the children of a 'mistress', brought up round the corner from the 'legitimate family'.

Media emperor Rupert Murdoch has this placement, and he created his very own toxic, complex family, pitting his children against each other in a battle for succession. This is one of the points in a chart where we look for inheritance and legacy. Interestingly, Murdoch was also born with the asteroid of inheritance Vesta rising, so clearly this is of great concern to him. Perhaps that is why he hung on to the reins of power for so long.

On a much more positive note, Lilith on the IC may show an adoption — and there is no need to assume this was a negative outcome. It could also suggest that you come from a family that was either forced to flee or chose to leave their native country, and again, this could have been the best choice at the time. You may in later life give shelter to waifs and strays. I have one person on my books with this placement who fosters dogs.

As always with astrology, there is a polarity here. So you may either have sense of deep rootedness with the Earth herself with this placement, or deracination.

Questions to ask yourself with this placement are: where do I feel safe? Was my family crazy, disrupted or just wildly original and liberated? Where are my roots? Can I create roots? Do I need multiple ways of connecting with my foundations?

Fifth House

Children, playfulness, pleasure, leisure, creativity, acting, theatre, drama, love affairs, flirtation, flings, sports, sex.

Find your Lilith in your children, your pleasures, your self-expression, or the way you play.

Lilith in the fifth house often simply lends a person uninhibited creativity. Several artists, actors and athletes on my books have this placement — and the more cutting edge their art the better. I've also seen this in the charts of people who are creative with the things of Lilith, or who pursue unusually interesting sex lives.

In short Lilith here is often free to roam and have fun.

Two of cinema's greatest martial artists — Jackie Chan and Bruce Lee — have Lilith in the fifth house, which is quite intriguing when you consider that the fifth is the house of theatre. Chan's is in Libra, the sign of partnership — and indeed, he often plays with a sidekick. In the Rush Hour movies, his co-star was Chris Tucker, who also happens to have Lilith in Libra. The one and only Bruce Lee in contrast, has Lilith in fierce Aries (*Enter the Dragon*, *Fist of Fury*), Libra's opposite sign. Both men are outrageously acrobatic, pushing martial arts in the movies to the limits of possibility, and in the case of Chan, to comedic effect: remember Lilith loves comedy. The fifth is, after all, the house of fun, where we go to disport ourselves.

Fifth house Lilith may be an outrageous showman — or woman. The singers Rihanna Fenty and Harry Styles, both famous for their flamboyance and sexiness, have this placement, and both are also noted fashion icons. Fashion at its most iconic is, of course, performance and play. There are

> "Besides which, she would never understand me because I like too many things and get all confused and hung-up running from one falling star to another till I drop. This is the night, what it does to you. I had nothing to offer anybody except my own confusion."
>
> — Jack Kerouac, *On the Road*

Fertility and Creativity

Lilith, according to legend, is both tremendously fertile herself, and a devourer of children and slayer of women in childbirth. In this she embodies some of the greatest fears that women have had for millennia.

Until very modern times, a woman's chance of surviving childbirth was uncertain. Both my own grandmothers were nearly killed by the processes of pregnancy and childbirth — and this is not at all unusual. The possibility of stillbirth, miscarriage and infant death was also high. In much of the world, beyond the reach of modern medicine, these dangers are still real. Amulets warding off Lilith or multiple Liliths during the precarious moment when life comes into the world have been found in Europe and Asia.

Some people choose not to have children and some people can't have children. Astrologically, this can look the same. Lilith may be in the fifth house of children natally, or conjunct the Moon or Sun when a person does not have children. I have seen transits of Lilith during abortion and miscarriage also.

Infertility treatment, with its intense medical intervention, still falls for the most part to women. In itself, the treatment can be a heroic quest, and may be part of the Lilith archetype of multiple births and deaths.

The other fears embodied in Lilith are of giving birth too much — too many mouths to feed, endless childbirth, endless breast-feeding. One of my clients born on the New Moon in Scorpio has a massive stellium in that sign. Her Sun-Moon conjunction is directly opposite Lilith in Taurus, one of the most fecund signs. She falls pregnant almost as easily as breathing and had four children before her first Saturn Return at age 28, as well as several miscarriages. This has, obviously, defined the shape of her life.

plenty of other singers and actors with Lilith here too. Bono, Robbie Williams, and Janis Joplin, who unsurprisingly had a conjunction of Lilith and an exalted expansive Jupiter in emotional Cancer here.

We can't all be stars though, and Lilith in the fifth does work in other ways, too.

This can be the place where Lilith shows herself as the mistress of miscarriage. One of my clients has Lilith in Capricorn on the cusp of her fifth house. She had five miscarriages, some very late. This is Lilith as the thief of children, or rescuer, perhaps, of infant souls. My client's Lilith makes an exact trine to Pluto, the Lord of the Underworld, in Virgo. Unsurprisingly, these experiences changed her profoundly. You will be glad to read that she did have a baby who is a grown man now. What is more, their relationship is exceptionally strong and deep.

I have come across many women who have had trouble having children with Lilith in the fifth, but this is not a hard and fast rule. Sometimes this is an indicator of no children, but you'd need to look in other places for this to be confirmed. After all, Rihanna has had no trouble making babies. It can also tell you what kind of child you might have — wild, talented, edgy.

Lilith is associated with sex, and there are two astrological houses where she can play more uninhibitedly with themes of sexuality — the fifth and the eighth. Lilith can be kinky, and in the fifth she may show an inclination to threesomes, or three way relationships. I've known people with Lilith here, who prefer to be the bit on the side because it comes with no strings, and they can indulge their fantasies. For some, unconventional sex can be a hobby.

Some questions to ask yourself with this placement. How do I define fun? How do I feel about children? How do I express myself? How am I creative? How can I go out of bounds? How do I feel about sex?

Sixth House

Work, routine, ritual, habit, quotidian life, schedules, duties, responsibilities, employees (traditionally servants), health, fitness.

Your Lilith may manifest in outré colleagues. Instead, bring her to work yourself.

You can imagine that some people with this placement literally work with Lilith. This may be as a magician working with dark matter and mystery like Nikola Tesla, the electrical engineer who predicted wireless communications, or film director Stephen Spielberg who conjured ET and Indiana Jones out of the darkness, or the early 20th-century psychic Edgar Cayce, or the author Stephen King, who sits down with Lilith at his desk every day and makes up scary stories. King is one of many authors with Lilith close to the Descendant, which divides the sixth from the seventh house. His Lilith in the sixth house of work is also incredibly prolific, giving birth to hundreds of novels and stories.

Lilith here can also tell us the kind of people we work with. Edgar Cayce did a lot of work with people who were unwell, or whom the medical profession had given up on. In other words, they had been cast out. The Indian statesman and philosopher, Mahatma Gandhi, had Lilith here — and of course he famously worked with Lilith's people, the Dalit community of India. The Dalits, so-called 'Untouchables', were considered polluted by other groups in India. It was left to them to deal with garbage, death and disease. This concept of pollution is a crucial one in the Lilith archetype.

Very occasionally, Lilith in the sixth tells you something about your own health. There may be a chronic condition that marginalises you.

Jagged Little Pill

Canadian singer songwriter Alanis Morissette has Lilith in the sixth close to the Descendant also. Her breakthrough album *Jagged Little Pill* — which sounds superbly furious — was recorded as Lilith cruised through her tenth house of fame by transit, and it was released in June 1994 as Lilith conjoined her wordsmithing Gemini Sun.

Lilith here can also lead you to a daily relationship with the things of Lilith, including a need to work with the natural world, for example in forestry. A person with the placement could do well to make sure that they get a daily dose of wildness, even if that's just going to the top of the building and feeling the wind. You may also find people who work with abortion, miscarriage or birth with this placement.

Quite a lot of outstanding sportspeople have this Lilith too, as Lilith can show an outrageous talent, and here she works through the physical body. Both Lionel Messi and Zinedine Zidane, two of Europe's finest 21st century footballers, have Lilith here. On the other side of that coin, there can be a dangerous relationship with the body, pushing it too far.

There is often something especially witchy about sixth and twelfth-house Lilith. These are people who see Lilith every day. You may have an unusual job that makes you stand outside society — astrologer or ethnographer or pole dancer.

Cook on the Wild Side

In the year 2000, a collection of essays called *Kitchen Confidential: Adventures in the Culinary Underbelly* became an international bestseller. It contained a gripping account of working as a chef in New York City. Its author, Anthony Bourdain, a charismatic storyteller, was immediately snapped up by television. His show *Parts Unknown* was a compelling combination of journalism, advocacy, travelogue and food fandom. You can see, simply by the titles, that Bourdain worked in the realms of Lilith.

His sixth house Lilith also manifested in other ways too. He was quite a serious drug addict for long stretches of his adult life and had a two-pack a day smoking habit too. That can be a danger of Lilith in the sixth. The daily dance with death can work well if you're writing horror novels, or rescuing animals or people, but you need to be careful about what you put in your own body.

Bourdain used his huge platform to passionately advocate for people and places that were not on the track beaten by American media. His fascination with food and cooking gave him entry into places that other journalists could not reach. The rest of Bourdain's chart synchs with these themes also, obviously. But Lilith in the sixth shows us his interest in working with outsiders, as well as pushing the limits of his own body.

Seventh House

Partners, friends, lovers, rivals, enemies, competitors, spouses

Find your Lilith in a partner, hold them close and transform them into a best beloved.

Lilith in the seventh may show an attraction to misfits, crazies, creative powerhouses, wild, wild women (and men), damaging people.

Or you may be an observer of Lilith, since the seventh can literally be what you look at in life, or what you like to look at. You often find that authors with this placement write about the things of Lilith. For example, Albert Camus, the French existentialist, has Lilith right on the Descendant. His most renowned books are named after Lilith: *The Outsider* and *The Plague*. The protagonist in *The Outsider* is certainly an avatar of Lilith's negative side — a cold-hearted, amoral killer, outside society, literally.

American beat poet Jack Kerouac also has this placement. His most famous work *On The Road* is about casting himself out of society, being on the edge. It's a story about travelling, and about a relationship between Sal Paradise, the narrator, and his friend, the fascinating Dean Moriarty. We see America and Dean through Sal's eyes, and eventually understand that Dean's art is to live life fully, and Sal's art is to bear witness, to write.

Charlotte Brontë's eponymous heroine Jane Eyre goes through the trials of Lilith — abandoned, cast out, unloved until she meets a male Lilith in the form of Mr Rochester. She is alone and without family. But what's particularly fascinating about this novel is Lilith in the attic, the first Mrs Rochester: the madwoman unresolved. Brontë has Lilith exactly on the Descendant, like Camus and Kerouac. She is an observer of Lilith. Brontë was writing as the Industrial Revolution tore into the heart of the English countryside; at a time when women were still unable to live freely, when choices for employment were limited for the most part to working as a governess, sewing, laundry or prostitution. With such limitations, Lilith bursts out passionately. In particular, Jane Eyre is an intelligent, independent woman trapped in a society where she will always be seen as spare. Not until she finds Lilith and marries him is she free.

Barack Obama's Significant Other

Barack Obama, twice-elected US President (2008-2016), has both Mean and True Lilith in the seventh house of partnerships. In fact, he has a stellium, which means a whole host of planets, in Leo here which runs from Mercury at 2° Leo to the North Node at 27° Leo; it includes his Sun and Uranus too. At the centre of this stellium is the Mean Lilith, the one that we generally use. But Obama's True Lilith is here too, making an exact conjunction with Mercury the communicator. Now, Obama's talent as a speaker is extraordinary, an almost supernatural ability to find the right words plus perfect pitch and timing. He was no slouch at writing either, penning volumes of autobiography before he was elected.

His Sun is the middle of the *Via Lamia* in the seventh house of partners. It's almost impossible to think of Barack Obama without Michelle, his wife, who was at first characterised as 'an angry black woman', which could be one description of Lilith herself. His people thought Michelle was not an asset initially and tried to keep her in the background, but over his presidency Michelle was transformed into one of the most-liked First Ladies in US history, and one who was able to implement some actual transformation, or at least plant a vegetable garden in the White House lawn. This is a journey from outcast to most beloved, which is possible with powerful Lilith placements when they are met, acknowledged and celebrated. Michelle became one of Barack Obama's greatest assets — indeed the strength of their partnership (a seventh house thing) was a powerfully positive role model. The fact that Barack Obama seemed to be such a loyal, devoted and equal partner to his wife won him many fans.

And yet, if we are to believe the negative stories of Lilith, it should have been the other way round. Why does Lilith work for Obama?

I think this is to do with being outcast. Obama is, in some ways, the complete outsider himself: with a white mother and an African father, he would never fit neatly into an American racial pigeonhole. He was neither a boy from the hood, nor a WASP. So he had a choice, embrace one or the other. Go towards Lilith, the 'angry black woman' or away from her. By going towards her, he became much more powerful and found his own unique way — which is the job of all Leos, of course. Leos must embrace their uniqueness in order to be happy, and with Lilith here, that uniqueness had to include some of that Lilith archetype; in the seventh house, it had to be in the form of partnership.

With this powerful archetype in the seventh, you have a chance to actively seek out Lilith — and reader, you might marry him. Indeed, this is often a wonderful placement for someone who marries outside the tribe.

The Descendant

The Descendant, which is the cusp of the seventh house, sitting directly opposite to the Ascendant, is one of the most important angles in your chart. It shows directly how you relate to others, who you seek out in partnership and what type of person is attracted to you. It can also show the style of partnership you like.

The rest of the seventh house adds detail and nuance to the initial pitch from the descendant. This is traditionally the house of marriage — and certainly shows the kind of spouse you may end up with. But it also shows other kinds of partnerships — friends, business partners, often siblings too, allies, clients, and rivals.

The closer Lilith is to your Descendant, the more directly she speaks to you. You are likely to come across her in the form of an enemy or a rival at different points in your life. You may need to recognise a jealous, unreasonable frenemy is holding up a mirror to your self. And this is one of the great advantages of Lilith in the seventh house: it gives you an opportunity to understand your own Lilith through your relationships and the people you encounter.

Consciously taking back your own projections and ceasing to blame others will liberate you, and allow you to work creatively with that powerful Lilith placement. Who is your inner Heathcliff? Who is your Dean Moriarty?

Lilith can also describe the kind of relationship you fall into sometimes — crazy, passionate, unbounded, sexy, ferocious, hungry, life-changing. And, in a way, that is truly enviable: to be able to fall deeply, truly, madly in love, is also in the realm of Lilith.

Eighth House

Taboo, sex, shared values, other people's money, psychology, secrets, debts, desire, death.

Find your Lilith in private, in the closest exchanges with another person.

It could be that Lilith rather enjoys being in the eighth house — after all, she is the Queen of Taboo, and this is where your secrets are hiding.

This can be an alluring placement that hints of danger and sex. It's notable that some of the 20th and 21st centuries biggest sex symbols — the King himself, Elvis Presley, and film stars Brigitte Bardot, Angelina Jolie, Sophia Loren, Catherine Zeta-Jones, Alexander Skarsgard and Ryan Gosling to name just a few — host Lilith in the eighth house of desire. This placement can bring a whiff of brimstone and edginess. It's notable that Skarsgard and Jolie excelled when they played unhinged characters. Jolie's breakout role was in *Girl Interrupted*, a film largely set in an asylum, and Skarsgard won a clutch of awards when he played an abusive husband in the miniseries *Big Little Lies* in the mid-teens. Both parts hint of the wildness of Lilith unleashed. Zeta-Jones has been very open about her own bipolar disorder.

But there is another kind of allure — the ability to magic money out of other people's wallets and into your own. Jeff Bezos, founder of Amazon and one of the richest men in the world, has Lilith in the eighth. In fact, this is one of the most obvious wealth indicators in his chart, which is actually more focused on status and power than money.

Often it's not as clearly defined when it comes to those of us who are not on the silver screen. It's a whisper of naughty but nice rather than a shout. This is also a place of concealment, so if you have Lilith here, you may be able to keep the wilder shores of your psyche effectively hidden. I've seen this in the charts of people who have had some racy periods in their lives, but prefer to keep that very private.

And there is another important factor to note about this placement. This is the house of death, and there can be something extraordinary or outré about how a person with this placement passes, or about their relationship with death itself.

Nineties soul diva Whitney Houston drowned in a bath tub at the Beverley Hills Hotel. She was born with an exact conjunction of Neptune, the Lord of the Sea, and Lilith in the eighth house. Neptune is also associated with glamour, music and drugs — all of which Houston had in excessive amounts. In particular, she was blessed with an almost outlandish talent for music. Remember that Lilith can show us where we excel or exceed normal limitations, when combined with an outer planet this can become overwhelming. Houston's Lilith was in Scorpio, a sign which can take a morbid interest in the dark. Despite her rough private life, from the outside for many years Houston was able to maintain a rather wholesome image. This could also be an eighth house feature: this is the house of secrets after all. And like Jeff Bezos, Houston was able to make phenomenal amounts of money. In the late 90s, she signed one of the biggest recording deals of all time.

If you host Lilith in this part of your chart, you may want to examine your relationship with money, sex and even crime. What are the secrets you keep? This house can also tell us something about what we have inherited or what resources we share. I have seen Lilith here when people have had a struggle around joint resources. For example, one of my collaborators went through a nasty divorce, and part of the difficulty was to do with the money her husband had hidden. This was part of a repeating pattern, since in her own family there was hidden wealth.

And this is the thing about any natal placement. It can reveal a pattern that repeats itself in various slightly different ways through your life. Once you see it you will be able to respond more effectively, and sooner, when it starts to unfold again.

This is also a house of debt — both in the fiscal sense and the moral or social one. You may find yourself on occasion in hock to someone unreasonable, or like another collaborator of mine, the inheritor of a debt.

This is also about worth, which may be more to do with how you feel your family or your partner is valued. So for example, like some of my clients, you may feel that you are descended from the 'poor relations' side of the family.

Ninth House

Philosophy, value systems, politics, publishing, broadcasting, travel, higher education, libraries, universities, organised religion, sharing of knowledge.

Find your Lilith on your travels to far away places, or by learning about or teaching wild, exotic Lilith topics such as feminism, refugee studies or forestry. Your Lilith may express itself when you speak to a crowd.

If you have Lilith in this sector, you could find yourself travelling to exotic or dangerous places, or you may have interesting or groundbreaking ideas that you want to share. After all, this is one of the communications houses — along with the third and to some extent the eleventh.

The ninth is the house of philosophy, organised religion, ideologies. So perhaps it's not surprising that a lot of politicians have this placement, including the late British Prime Minister Margaret Thatcher and Turkey's President Recep Erdoğan — two people with strong ideas that changed the course of their country's histories.

Another aspect of this placement that's pretty useful for politicians is charisma, an ability to charm a crowd. You see it in the charts of quite a few stadium-filling frontmen and women — Coldplay's Chris Martin, Led Zeppelin's Jimmy Page, Radiohead's Thom Yorke, Erykah Badu. This is because we're approaching the point of fame, the Midheaven, which divides the ninth from the tenth house. Mind you, even more very famous people seem to have Lilith in the tenth than the ninth. But you'll notice that even these rockers have something to impart, something to say.

It may be a nastier side of Lilith that brings you to the attention of the media. Here are three famous examples: remember that Lilith is associated with sexual transgression. Harvey Weinstein, the American film producer convicted on numerous counts of rape; Ghislaine Maxwell, the British heiress convicted of sex trafficking children; and Polish film director Roman Polanski convicted *in absentia* for having sex with a minor.

Martin Luther King's *Via Lamia*

American civil rights leader Martin Luther King was an extraordinary speaker; one reason for this was that his ideas had a strong philosophical basis. King was not just speaking from a place of anger or even as a reporter on the injustice that he saw all around him, he was speaking from a place of deep cogitation, and his ideas were systematic and organised.

King's *Via Lamia* spans the eighth and ninth houses of his natal chart, the houses of death and philosophy. It's a pretty wide road, spanning from Sagittarius to Capricorn.

His writing and speech-making was a ninth house activity. This is where we share our ideas, and King's ideas were about 'outsiderism', which is the realm of Lilith. In fact, you could argue that racist language about Africans and Black Americans did and still often does use the same descriptors as Lilith: savage, unruly, angry, unclean, sexually available or voracious. These are words used about out-groups everywhere, and about Lilith. Lilith is the outsider, and Dr King was philosophising and speaking about just these concepts.

But, as with all archetypes, there is at least one other side to this. He was shot down on 4 April 1968 while standing on the balcony of his hotel. Lilith by transit had entered his first house and trined his Sun, but perhaps the Lilith in the eighth house of death in the sign of Sagittarius, the archer, warned of such an ending.

This house is also associated with further education, and you may have some difficulty here with this placement — or become an expert in a Lilith subject: for example, feminism, refugee studies, botany, gynaecology, sex education. Lilith here can help you to break the boundaries of a subject.

A notable example of Lilith in the ninth house is the novelist Salman Rushdie. He was already a best-selling author when his magical realist novel *The Satanic Verses* was published in 1989. Some people found its subject extremely offensive — it broke one taboo too many — and Rushdie had to go into hiding. Since its publication he has survived multiple attempts on his life. In 2022, Rushdie was about to give a public talk. He was stabbed nearly to death on stage in front of an audience. On that day, Lilith was exactly opposing her own position in Rushdie's natal chart.

Tenth House

Career, status, public image, public influence.

Find your Lilith in your public life or your vocation.

The 10th house Lilith is hard to hide. You may be celebrated for some kind of Lilith type activity — confounding the bourgeoisie, living in the wild, being a rock and roll star. Unsurprisingly, a lot of celebrities have this placement, especially movie stars. Lilith can give your public image an edge of danger, sexiness, threat that is just so alluring.

The downside is that you might find yourself embroiled in a scandal, or falsely suspected of being some kind of scarlet lady or gentleman. The same can be true of ninth house Lilith close to the Midheaven. This can be a tricky placement. I've known people with this one who really found themselves dragged into a mess that was not of their own making, victims of slander.

However, to work with this Lilith you do need to let her out and allow her to roam around a little. One way of doing this, as all those movie stars can testify, is to perform Lilith. Another way is to have a Lilith career — feminist, activist, advocate for the underdog or the outcast. You might be a historian of oppression, a journalist who reports from refugee camps, or conservationist working in the wild. You really can't ignore this Lilith placement.

Lilith on the Midheaven

When I was thinking of modern embodiments of the Lilith archetype, an example of Lilith taking over and possibly overpowering the rest of the chart, the image of late British soul singer Amy Winehouse came instantly to mind: in her dripping makeup, with her monstrous hair, awkward in her tattoos and mini-skirt; her immortal, ancient voice. Winehouse's personal style was distinctive — messy, sexy, dark, dirty. Her voice was incredible: husky, smoky, from another place. She seemed at once very young, yet possessed by an eldritch spirit. Her songs — 'Back to Black', 'Rehab' — spoke of self destruction, being cast out of love, despair. She was crucified by the tabloid press and public hunger. I'll never forget her set at Glastonbury in 2008 when she tottered on to the stage and the audience howled. It was a terrifying display of talent and damage rolled up in one person, of audience and artist connecting emotionally — and of the sacrifice of an artist by the mob, like some strange ancient ritual.

So in a way, it came as no surprise when I looked up Winehouse, and found that in her natal chart, Lilith sits on her Midheaven. The Midheaven astrologically is our public image, what we are seen as. Winehouse was a public embodiment of Lilith, acting her out on the stage for the rest of the world to devour.

Poetic Delirium

"I turned silences and nights into words. What was unutterable, I wrote down. I made the whirling world stand still."

Thus wrote French poet Arthur Rimbaud, who was born with Lilith on his Midheaven, and the *Via Lamia* in the ninth house. Rimbaud's entire life seems in some ways to have been an exploration of his own ninth house Lilith from different angles.

He was a precocious talent, writing one of his most admired poems, 'The Drunken Boat', at the age of 16 in 1870. The poem, which would become one of the central works of the Symbolist movement, describes the travels of an empty vessel — again the Lilith theme of void. A few months later he was embarking on what would become an infamous drug-fuelled affair with the poet Paul Verlaine, which ended with the latter shooting him in the wrist in a Brussels hotel. During much of the affair, Rimbaud was experiencing a Lilith Return, and poetry was pouring out of him. Meanwhile his contemporaries described him as dirty and rude, a scandalous *enfant terrible* — a perfect description of one kind of Lilith in Cancer, the sign of children. But suddenly the flow of gorgeous, effulgent poetry stopped when he was just 21 in 1875. Even so, he had changed the idea of what poetry could be with his prose poems, and unknowingly started the Symbolist movement. Rimbaud's Lilith though had other work in mind. He travelled, as far afield as Java, eventually settling in Yemen, where he became a trader. Rimbaud was one of only three foreigners to reside in Harar, fulfilling that other Lilithian destiny: being an outsider.

Carl Jung's *Via Lamia*

Carl Jung, the father of depth psychology, whose work with the dark feminine influenced generations of writers, movie-makers, myth-weavers, has one of the widest *Via Lamias* possible. It spans the whole of the tenth house — spreading from his Mean Lilith smack on the Midheaven, right through to the True Lilith in the eleventh house of futurism, where it makes a conjunction with the action planet Mars. Jung, of course, did not work with the Dark Moon Lilith. It had not really come into the astrological mainstream when he was working, but you could say that his insight that we all contain a dark other, a shadow, is precisely an expression of Lilith, and influenced his whole life, and his work. Maybe this was most obvious in his work on the *anima* — the female part of a man's soul.

On a more mundane level, he paraded his affair with fellow psychoanalyst Toni Wolff, turning his marriage into a three-way relationship for years. This is classic Lilith in the tenth behaviour — outrageous and in plain sight. Wolff's Lilith was also in the tenth house. She was a close colleague of Jung's as well as his lover and helped him develop the theory of the *anima*, the other. Tellingly, her Lilith makes an exact conjunction with Jung's wife Emma's Jupiter, the magnifier, right on Emma's Descendant, the place of the other, the husband or rival. Jung's Pluto is just a degree from this spot. It's hard not to imagine that there was a certain amount of emotional cruelty involved, as well as sexual obsession. All these planets are in the sexy sign of Taurus.

Which set me thinking about others who might have this same signature, yet act it out in different and less personally harmful ways. If you have Lilith on your Midheaven, you will have to grapple with public perception of you as a type of Lilith — even if this is very far from the truth of yourself.

Horror maestro Vincent Price, who played so many sinister, scheming, charming villains in movies also had Lilith on his Sagittarian Midheaven. Watching him in his first big horror role in *House of Wax* (1953) it's easy to see how he channels that dark power in his performance. This unsettling ability to strike fear into his audience stood him in good stead through his entire career, and funded his fine art collection.

The infamous Marquis de Sade, author of *120 Days of Sodom*, is a less wholesome example of Lilith on the Midheaven perhaps. It's in Leo, the sign of drama. The 18th century aristocrat, writer, pornographer, rapist and child abuser is the reason we have the word 'sadist', a person who enjoys inflicting pain.

Lilith on the Midheaven can be channeled into performance. And this can work very well. Indeed a lot of rockers have a powerful Lilith. For example, Peter Gabriel, political activist and rock and roll superstar, has the same Lilith as Amy Winehouse. One of his biggest hits is an invitation to fornication, because he's like a 'sledgehammer'. Guitar god Jimmy Page of Led Zeppelin fame also has a highly-placed Lilith, conjoining the North Node and approaching the Midheaven.

But there are other ways that this Lilith appears. I have a client who began her career specialising in massage for pregnant women, but her practice grew from there to coaching women through becoming mothers, and then through menopause. She sees herself as working with thresholds and initiation, bringing women from one stage of life to the next. Her Lilith is as strongly placed as Amy Winehouse's, but it is in Aries, the sign of beginnings. Mind you, she is known as something of a witch.

So if your Lilith is in the tenth, and especially if it is near the Midheaven, you will have no choice but to grapple with her, embrace her and understand that for some people you will likely embody her. It's a matter of making sure that the Lilith you embody is the positive one, not the Lilith who brings shame.

Eleventh House

Groups, societies, audiences, corporations, wishes, hopes and dreams, social networks, politics.

Find your Lilith in the crowd or outside the crowd, locate your audience.

This can be an especially potent place to host Lilith, since she is the goddess of outcasts and this is the land of the group. You may find yourself, therefore, an outsider, or hanging out with outsiders. You may work with refugees, migrants, the homeless or people who, in some other way, find themselves on the margins of society.

On a completely different note, you may mingle with the outrageous or flamboyant others. Maybe your job is to shock the bourgeoisie as, say, a drag queen or performance artist.

A really notable example of the eleventh house Lilith is Kim Kardashian (see also Lilith in Libra). Rich, handsome and clever, Kardashian has made a fortune by selling women a little essence of herself. She was certainly one of the greatest influencers of the early 21st century, selling herself, her lifestyle and her products on Instagram and in her reality TV shows *The Kardashians* and *Keeping Up With the Kardashians*. Along with her family, her cultural impact across the globe has been extremely powerful. Her self-presentation is in some ways high camp, an exaggerated version of Los Angeles rich girl.

She has weaponised her private life to create a public persona that is intensely alluring. She turned out to be relatable for a huge global audience. At the same time, there is something of the outsider about Kim. She's not black, and often gets accused of cosplaying blackness; at the same time, she is not vanilla. She also is in herself a corporation, a company.

So, not only does Kardashian have Lilith in the eleventh house of audiences, it is in exact conjunction with Pluto, the planet of vast wealth, and in the sign of Libra, which is associated with beauty and the beauty industry.

This is, of course, an extreme example of Lilith in the eleventh, but there's one final note on this: Kim Kardashian's ex, Kanye West, also has Lilith in the 11th — and he's leveraged that in a different way. Some would suggest that he's leveraged his 'crazy' to create an audience. Another aspect of his Lilith in the eleventh is his legendary inability to work with teams. Apparently, when he had a collaboration with sportswear maker Adidas they had to have a special human resources person to support personnel assigned to West.

Even those of us who are not world-famous need to acknowledge Lilith when she is in the eleventh. This is not a Lilith that can be safely closeted. You will need to meet her as a public part of yourself — whether that means you're the only person wearing the hijab in your school, or the only person going bareheaded. You'll need to embrace your difference, and find your tribe of fellow outsiders.

Another example of someone who embraced his inner outsider is the late-lamented English rock star David Bowie aka Ziggy Stardust, aka Aladdin Sane, aka The Thin White Duke. Bowie experimented with many personae throughout his career, but even at his most weird and distant, he struck a chord with a massive audience. He plugged straight in to everyone's feeling of alienation and acted it out for the rest of us. Bowie's Lilith saw him strutting the stage in gender-defying knitwear, dying his hair red, pink, orange, singing like a glorious banshee, and experimenting endlessly. One of the things I associate with Lilith is tremendous creativity when she is active. Bowie was extraordinarily inventive, Kanye West is touted as a 'creative genius', and Kim Kardashian has led the march in an entire way of being and marketing in the 21st century.

During his infamous Berlin years, strung out on heroin, living on the edge of the divided city, Bowie produced three of his greatest albums, and found important collaborators — Brian Eno, Iggy Pop, Robert Fripp. And in this, his career really holds a secret for those of us with this Lilith placement: sometimes it pays to choose exile — at least for a while. He came back to London, eventually in triumph, and reinvented himself again. He found his eventual home on the other side of the Atlantic though. In New York City, he found he could be anonymous. Absenting yourself from the herd does not have to be forever, but it could help you to step outside of your group for a while and look back in, critically. This is true professionally too. I have a vet on my books who spends a few weeks every year looking after animals in the global South. This is incredibly beneficial for her practice back in the North.

Of course, there is a downside. There always is. The French queen beheaded at the guillotine during the French Revolution, Marie Antoinette, also has this placement. Her Lilith is in a sign of consumption, Taurus. She was extremely unpopular before the uprising, seen as a greedy, foreign interloper — almost literally Lilithed by the mob — and blamed for the decadence of the French Court. In other words, the audience, the people, the crowds can turn against you, and burn you like a witch at the stake.

With Lilith here you might ask yourself: who is my crowd? Who is my audience? How do I fit in? When do I need to be "other"?

Twelfth House

Dreams, imagination, collective unconscious, popularity of a kind, mental health, emotional inheritance, ancestors, spiritual guardians.

Find Lilith in your dreams, the story of your family or even in the deep past.

This most mysterious of houses is the final one in our string of pearls around the horoscope. Like the eighth house, even astrologers have trouble pinning down exactly what it means. In traditional astrology, it has quite a bad reputation: it's known as the house of self-undoing, or the house of loss. Vedic astrologers associate this place with the bedroom, the most private place in the home. This house is the gateway into and connection with the collective unconscious, and Lilith can be a key.

For me, it's important to really listen to a client with planets in this house and unravel the meaning with them. I have noticed that they often literally represent ancestors — and with Lilith here that ancestor may have been a refugee, had mental health problems, or been a medicine woman or cunning man.

Lilith in the twelfth can indicate an indefinable allure, and create seemingly immortal popularity. Many really huge stars have this placement. The singer-songwriter Taylor Swift has a *Via Lamia* through the 12th which embraces her Pluto in Scorpio. Of course, she has a spooky knack for connecting with her audience, but Swift also has seemingly limitless imagination. Much of it is focused around that Pluto in Scorpio — sex, jealousy.

There is a shadowy feel to the twelfth house. This is the realm of the unconscious, and it can be hard to work consciously with Lilith when she lives here. You may have to seek her out in your dreams or daydreams, in your family tree. The closer she is to your Ascendant, the more likely you are to feel her breathing on the back of your neck.

This vast imaginative resource is evident in the work of JK Rowling, creator of Harry Potter and an entire fantasy universe, where reality and magic co-exist. Harry Potter — orphaned, outcast, scarred, humiliated — is, to some extent, an avatar of Lilith. Rowling's own natal Lilith is in the twelfth in Aquarius, the sign of everyman or woman, directly opposite her creative Leo Sun. Potter was the secret version of herself that she saw in the mirror, a lonely single mother sitting in a greasy spoon in Edinburgh. Rowling saw her own Lilith, a young boy fighting injustice, and wrote him down.

I have come across Lilith here for several people who have had long periods of seclusion or exclusion. This has been due to illness — mental or physical — or family or tribal rupture. By that last, I mean, people who have had to flee their place of birth because they don't fit in politically or because of their sexual orientation, for example. It can feel as if you are tossed into the void for a while, but this is often an experience that happens once, is formative, and then as you grow you resolve it and become the person you were supposed to be.

After encountering your own Lilith in this house, you may find that she really "has your back". She may be like a secret ally or coach. Just make sure that she is motivating you to create, engage with the "other", explore the wilder edges of your own imagination, and not encouraging you to go hog wild! The key is recognition.

Part III

THE BEAUTIFUL WOMAN SOOTHES THE SERPENT-KING

Loving Your Wild Self

All the tales of Lilith which you have read in these pages so far should be starting to coalesce in your own imagination. Some stories you will doubtless identify with, and some will seem far away.

Now it's time to look in the mirror at your own Lilith. You will never tame her, of course, but you might just make friends with her. The better you know her, the more you might like her. And if you love your wild self, she may turn out to be your greatest supporter, your muse and your protector.

Making Sense

Now we have met Lilith in the twelve houses and in the twelve signs it's time for you to integrate those two. Essentially, the house is the 'where and the sign is the 'how', but in order to blend those two you may want to think about how this works.

Remember that we are working with the Mean Lilith here. We'll talk more about True Lilith in a few pages.

There are some clear examples that you can ponder, which show up the contrast. Think about how both Marilyn Monroe and Mary Oliver share the same house placement — Lilith directly on the Ascendant — but how Lilith is expressed quite differently. Although both women are Lilith types, Monroe's is in fiery Leo, the sign of performance and uniqueness, whereas Oliver's is in earthy Virgo, a writer's sign.

Or say you have Lilith in Aquarius on the Descendant, the cusp of the seventh house. That certainly means you will encounter Lilith in your life through other people. You may end up in three-way relationships, but it's just as likely that you will marry outside the tribe, or find yourself fascinated by unusual people. You may create a group of friends — Aquarius — who you see regularly for one-to-ones when you do Lilith style things together.

Or say you have Lilith in the second house in Libra. What is your relationship with fairness (Libra)? And with earning a living? Do you earn a crust by defending outsiders? Or helping others to emotionally balance?

Or maybe you have Lilith in Sagittarius in the tenth. Have you found yourself the victim of outrageous (Sagittarius) publicity (tenth)?

Astrology is a subtle art. You can't use a blunt object to create this blending. Instead, dip your brush in the colours, blend them and see what shapes appear on your canvas.

The rest of your chart is, of course, key. So see how Lilith works with the other planets. You may find that the presence of Lilith will explain why, for example, that Sun in Leo is so very unusual. Actually, you have a wild streak thanks to a secret conjunction with Lilith. Oddly, I have several people on my books with a Sun-Lilith conjunction that is so close, we call it *cazimi,* in the heart of the Sun. All have led lives that are beautifully non-conformist. Each has taken the road less travelled. And in fact, all have thrived. They each followed Lilith. One of those is my dear mother, with Lilith in the heart of her Libra Sun. She was, to put it mildly, the black sheep of her family — artistic, bohemian, and from her mid-20s she always lived as a foreigner in a strange land.

If you are new to astrology, keep it simple. Integrate the sign and house placement in your mind, really familiarising yourself with how this may be working for you, and then move on to aspects with planets and angles. Only count the oppositions and conjunctions at first, and keep the orb reasonably tight too — no more than 5°. The most important planets to consider are Sun, Moon and the ruler of the chart, that is the planet that rules the sign on the Ascendant. But very tight aspects to any of the traditional planets (0°-2°) by Lilith are also significant — Mercury, Venus, Mars, Saturn and Jupiter, and the Nodes of the Moon. The same is true when Lilith nudges any of the four angles of the chart: Ascendant, Descendant, Midheaven and IC.

Lilith energises the planets and angles she touches. She gives them power and unpredictability. For example, I have a client with a beautifully placed Venus in Libra in the second. This should be lucky with income. It even trines Saturn, which is also lovely. So why has his income gone up and down so wildly? Venus is conjoined by Lilith. It was never going to be a straightforward accounting job — unless it was for the mafia.

So the question you may be asking is: how do I do my best by Lilith? The first thing is to acknowledge this part of your own psyche, or of your real lived experience. Reflect on your own history, how it works with the positive or negative aspects of your Lilith placement by sign and house. If you're deeper in astrology, consider Lilith's connections to your planets.

Transits of Lilith

Your personal astrology is not fixed but evolving. Your natal chart is based on the exact moment of your birth, but as you grow and the world turns, things move on. Your horoscope receives aspects by transit from the planets and points moving through the zodiac. For example, the Sun makes a transit through the entire zodiac over every 12-month period, starting at 0° Aries on the spring equinox and ending at 29°59' Pisces the following year on the day before. In contrast, the Moon transits through the entire zodiac every month over a period of 28 days.

All the other planets take differing lengths of time — from Pluto at over 200 years to Mercury at under 12 months — to make their way around the zodiac. As they do so, they will be making different geometrical patterns with your birth horoscope. We refer to these as transits.

The Moon's apogee takes nine years to pass through the whole zodiac, and nine months in each sign — about the length of a pregnancy. This means that Lilith will make meaningful aspects to all points in your chart, and return to where she was when you were born through the period of a decade.

Lilith's transits can be subtle but you may, for example, find yourself in a characteristically Lilith entanglement as she transits particular parts of the sky, especially if she activates existing patterns. You may find yourself cast out of a social group as she goes through your eleventh, or performing wild and outrageous music, or breaking free of an unbearable relationship when she reaches your first. For example, one client found herself caught in a three-way affair, when an ex-girlfriend turned out to be not so ex, as Lilith transited her seventh house of relationships.

Lilith transits to the Moon are especially significant. These can be full of emotional turmoil, or inner exploration. If you were born with this aspect you may find that your whole life takes on some Lilith tones. Several clients with this aspect had unusual mothers — mentally unstable, exiled from their nation, exiled from family, or simply fierce — or have had unusual experiences of parenting themselves.

As Lilith transits through the signs, notice how news related to Lilith themes comes and goes. For example, Lilith transited through Cancer in 2022 when long-held abortion rights in the United States were thrown out. The US is a Cancer nation, born on 4 July, so this transit activated the core identity, and Cancer is also the sign of mom and apple pie. Lilith is associated with abortion.

Your Lilith Cycle

All of us are born with the Black Moon Lilith somewhere in our charts, and all of us will have some of that energy playing out in our lives. Her power is stronger or weaker depending on her position and the aspects she makes with other planets and points — and it also waxes and wanes as she makes her way around the zodiac.

Your Lilith Return comes every nine years. This can be an important period for understanding just how Lilith works for you. Pay attention to the whole time that she's in your own Lilith sign. Equally important can be the year that Lilith opposes herself by sign. So for example, if you were born with Lilith in Leo, you should also be especially aware when Lilith makes her way through Aquarius.

And remember that your entire cohort is also having a Lilith Return with you.

Working Your Lilith

Unless you have a very prominent Lilith, she will sometimes be silent. In fact, your Lilith may not be much in evidence for years at a time. Don't force your Lilith into the open, and don't assume that she will conform to any stereotypes about the dark feminine, dark man, or dark anything. Each of us has our own expression of this energy. Coax her awake.

Where is it in your life that you feel unhinged? Or where do you feel constrained? And how do you express that part of yourself.

If you have found yourself wrestling with the more difficult aspects of this energy — self-harm, toxic relationships, inner turmoil, damaged people — consider how you could express Lilith in a less harmful way. Could you take your wildness into the woods? Or into the studio? Or the coven? Or into the boardroom to turn everything inside out?

Once you have read the previous section of this book, take some time to sit down with that Lilith, and enter an imaginary dialogue with her. How would she like to be part of your life? It may be through poetry, or long-distance running, or marrying a stranger. Have you met her in real life? Was she your sister who ran away? Or the best friend who runs an animal shelter? Don't forget that astrology manifests as both an inner experience and outer events. The more we can acknowledge the inner experience the easier the outer events can be to handle.

Clearly, we are all subject to the randomness of fate. You can't tell a person caught up in a war or an insurrection or a cancer treatment that it's the universe doing them a favour. What we can do is react to our circumstances in the least harmful and most effective way possible. Lilith, to a certain extent, is about randomness. This is not a rational energy. Lilith does not move step by step, instead she flaps her leathery wings, goes to sleep, wakes up with a bang. She is the essence of unpredictable, and this is part of your own nature too. Mind you, some people are a lot more cautious than others, and a lot less likely to fly off to the edge of the Red Sea.

Via Lamia

The cycle of Mean Lilith, is in fact very steady, and the True Lilith is very unsteady. So it's as if there is a still authentic centre to Lilith — the Mean Lilith — and a wild pulsing energy the swings out on a thread.

As you may have noticed reading the examples within these pages — some successful people have a highly focused Lilith, when Mean and True are close together, but equally some have a wide *Via Lamia*. Both can work, but the narrow Lilith is more obsessively focused, even their excess can be focused, whereas the wide *Via Lamia* may exhibit a much greater range of expression.

It's important to check your own *Via Lamia*, look at both ends of it — the Mean and True. If you have a very wide *Via Lamia*, you may well find that you span a couple of houses and a couple of signs. If this is the case, you will need to consider how both work.

So for example, you may have Mean Lilith in Aquarius in your sixth house and True Lilith in Pisces in your seventh house. This means the *Via Lamia* spans your Descendant, flavouring all your relationships; sometimes they are Aquarian — cool, friendly, constructive — and sometimes they are Pisces — deeply emotional and maybe manipulative. If the *Via Lamia* is in one house only, that makes interpretation easier, but if it spans two houses, that means several areas of your life will feel the Lilith. So in this example, you may find that you work with Lilith every day in the sixth house of routine which affects your job, and also that you have a one-to-one relationship with this energy in the seventh.

This may all seem complicated at first, but it will become clear, especially if you follow the transits of Lilith through your own houses in the horoscope.

Following Lilith's change of signs once a year will also highlight changes in the world — these may be natural, geo-political or cultural.

The key to working with Lilith is simple really: pay attention.

Part IV

Background

From Inanna to Baby Suggs, Heathcliff to Frank-N-Furter, Lady Macbeth to Lady Gaga, Kali to Kylie, Lilith runs like a glistening thread of spider's silk through culture. She, or sometimes he, is an irresistible, incorrigible, defiant, resilient character.

In this section you can read her evolution through Western culture, and find some more inspiration through books, films and art.

The Evolution of Lilith's Story

In Genesis, the first book of the Bible, God creates the world and everything in it, including the Sun and Moon, the sea and the land, the plants and animals, last of all He, and of course it is He, fashions a man from clay and calls him Adam. From Adam's rib, God creates a woman for him... or did he?

There is a Jewish legend that is not in the Bible, in which God created the very first woman from the same clay as Adam. Her name was Lilith and she came before Eve.

Currently, the earliest-known complete telling of the Jewish legend of Lilith is from *The Alphabet of Ben Sirach* or Sira, written anonymously somewhere in the Islamic world between 700 and 1000 AD. [6]

But there are many traces of Lilith that pre-date the *Alphabet*. It is fairly certain that the concept of Lilith — a child-killing, night-flying, seducer — is an ancient pre-Biblical one. Scholars trace the legend back to earlier tales of demonesses from Mesopotamia, and they don't all agree on where the story originated.

> *"O flyer in a dark chamber, go away at once, O Lili!"*[7]

This is from a 7th-century BC tablet found at Arslan Tash in northern Syria.

---

6 See Chapter One

7 translated from the ancient Phoenician-Canaanite dialect by William F. Albright. Patai, Raphael. *Lilith*. Vol.77, No. 306 Journal of American Folklore. Oct-Dec 1964

It is clear that Lilith was widely feared throughout the Near East[8] for millennia, as much of the evidence for belief in her consists of amulets of protection, especially for pregnant women and mothers. Babies were believed to be especially vulnerable to Lilith (death) in the first few weeks after being born. These amulets have been found from Iran to Southern Italy. Most are written invocations or imprecations. Many name the three angels who made a deal with Lilith, as Senoy, Sansenoy and Semangelof, or some equally sibilant variation on those names. Incantation bowls found dating from the Sassanid period (224-651 AD) in Iran were designed to catch the demoness before she could do any harm. At least one was made for a member of the Parsi religion, so belief in the demoness was not confined to Jews. Some bowls feature a wild-haired woman with a pronounced vagina encircled by magical words. In Alsatia and Switzerland, a Krassmesser, a type of magical knife, was used by Jewish people to draw a circle that kept out demons during childbirth.

Medieval Temptress

The Alphabet is quite tangential to Jewish tradition and could be described as satirical and definitely comical — Ben Sirach's many talents include curing farts for a princess — so as a source for the Lilith myth, it is odd, and perhaps that in itself is part of the Lilith archetype — always a little disreputable, a little surprising, disruptive. There is a bawdy character to this re-telling of the Lilith story that recalls another ancient tradition, the telling of lewd jokes which was part of the Eleusinian mysteries.[9] Lewdness,

---

8 "And I, the Instructor, proclaim His glorious splendour so as to frighten and to te[rrify] all the spirits of the destroying angels, spirits of the bastards, demons, Lilith, howlers, and [desert dwellers] ... and those which fall upon men without warning to lead them astray from a spirit of understanding and to make their heart and their ... desolate during the present dominion of wickedness and predetermined time of humiliations for the sons of lig[ht], by the guilt of the ages of [those] smitten by iniquity – not for eternal destruction, [bu]t for an era of humiliation for transgression." — Dead Sea Scrolls

9 At particular spot along the way to Eleusis, it was traditional to shout filthy jokes. This was in commemoration of Baubo or Iambe, who made the goddess Demeter laugh even while she was grief-stricken after the loss of her daughter Persephone.

"Till Iambe, who was knowing and careful, placed for her
A fixed seat, and draped a bright-shining fleece over it.
There she sat down, and held a veil in front of her.

coarse laughter and shock may be part of Lilith's armoury. Indeed, it was said that if a baby laughed in her sleep, it was a sign that Lilith was tickling her feet.[10]

After Ben Sirach, there seem to be quite a lot of references to Lilith in Kabbalistic writing, but accounts of her story vary and are fairly inconsistent. In the foundational Kabbalistic text, *The Zohar*, she is referred to as the lowest emanation (*sephiroth*) on the Tree of Death. Her legions of daughters are said to be terribly alluring and dangerous creatures. In the Talmud, people are warned not to sleep alone in the house at night, because you 'will be seized by the evil spirit Lilith.' [11] She is also specifically linked to the dark planet Saturn astrologically.[12] Saturn was the planet of melancholy, black bile, poverty and suffering according to astrologers of the Middle Ages. On a different note, in the 16th century Lurianic Kabbalah she is the wife of Adam Kadmon, the eternal light, or in contrast, the wife of Samael, Satan.

At the same time, it seems clear that although there are no known textual references to Lilith in Christian writing at this point, there was a tradition that the snake who tempted Eve in the Garden of Eden was female. There are many depictions of this moment, in which the snake

---

For a long time she sat on the couch without speaking, sorrowing,
Nor did she embrace anyone in word or deed,

But without laughing and not tasting food or drink
She sat wasting away in longing for her deep-girdled daughter,
Till Iambe, who was knowing and careful, with jests
Made many jokes and turned the mood of the divine lady,
By smiling and laughing, and keeping her heart gracious:
So she pleased the goddess afterwards with her kindly temperament."

From 'Homeric Hymns To Demeter'. Translated by Hugh G. Evelyn-White.

10 From the 16th century it was commonly believed that if an infant laughed in his sleep it was an indication that Lilith was playing with him, and it was therefore advisable to tap him on the nose to avert the danger (H. Vital, *Sefer ha-Likkutim* (1913), 78c; *Emek ha-Melekh*, 130b). *Encyclopedia Judaica*

11 Rabbi Ḥanina said: It is prohibited to sleep alone in a house, and anyone who sleeps alone in a house will be seized by the evil spirit Lilith. — Shabbat 151b *William Davidson Talmud*

12 "In the Kabbalah, Lilith is related to the planet Saturn, and all those of a melancholy disposition - of a 'black humor' - are her sons (Zohar, *Ra'aya Meheimna* III, 227b)" — *Encylopedia Judaica*

looks like a mirror image of Eve herself, and several of what looks like a love triangle between Adam, Eve and Lilith/Snake. On the western portal of the cathedral of Notre Dame in Paris there is a particularly beautiful carving of the scene with Lilith emerging from the Tree of Knowledge between Adam and Eve.

Obviously, Eve's original sin, that is accepting the apple from the Tree of Knowledge, was the basis for much misogyny in Christian culture. Eve's action became the action of all womankind. All women were blamed for the fall from grace, and this attitude permeated the whole culture, leading eventually, according to some historians, to the witch trials (c.1560-c.1750). Many of the accusations against the witches were identical to those levelled against Lilith herself — marriage to Satan, hyper-sexuality, seduction, shape-shifting, child-murder, abortion, miscarriage. The ancient Sumerian demoness re-emerged in the shape of a modern witch in the fevered imagination of Heinrich Kramer in the pages of *Malleus Maleficarum* (1486), *The Witch Hammer*. This was an incredibly influential book, a best-seller second only to the Bible itself through the 16th century. Kramer really hates women in general, reserving special loathing for women who have been cast out of the marital bed.

> "...when she hates someone whom she formerly loved, then she seethes with anger and impatience in her whole soul, just as the tides of the sea are always heaving and boiling. Many authorities allude to this cause. Ecclesiasticus xxv: There is no wrath above the wrath of a woman. And Seneca (Tragedies, VIII): No might of the flames or the swollen winds, no deadly weapon, is so much to be feared as the lust and hatred of a woman who has been divorced from the marriage bed."[13]

Lilith Reborn

A resurgence of literary and artistic interest in the story of Lilith began in the late 18th century, in parallel with a revival of interest in the Greek god of wild places, Pan.[14] Indeed, Lilith and Pan share many characteristics, although Lilith is almost always portrayed as having evil intent, whereas

---

13 Kramer, Heinrich. *Malleus Maleficarum*. Part I, Question VI.

14 Hutton, Ronald. *The Triumph of the Moon: A History of Modern Pagan Witchcraft*

Pan is morally ambiguous. Both are associated with unbridled desire, wild places, wild animals and wild behaviour.

It's clear that the story of Lilith as Adam's first wife was well-known. The German writer Goethe, possibly the most influential thinker in Europe at the time, refers to Lilith in his play *Faustus*. A complete version of Part One was published in 1809, although he had been working on it for several decades previously. In *Faustus*, Mephistopheles speaks of Lilith at the *Walpurgis Nacht*, the witch's night.

> "Adam's first wife. Of her rich locks beware!
> That charm in which she's parallel'd by few;
> When in its toils a youth she doth ensnare,
> He will not soon escape, I promise you."[15]

A decade later, in his bizarre and fascinating autobiography, published in 1818-1821, the French demonologist Berbiguier de Terre-Neuve du Thym describes the court in hell, which puts Lilith and Pan together as the sexy demons.

> "Princes and dignitaries.
> Beelzebuth, supreme chief; Satan dethroned prince, Eurynome, prince of death, Moloch, prince of the land of tears; Pluto prince of fire, Pan, prince of the Incubi, Lilith, prince of the Succubi, Leonard, grand master of the sabbath; Baalberith, grand pontif, Prosperine [Persephone], arch-demoness."[16]

15 von Goethe, Johann Wolfgang. *Faust — Part One*. Project Gutenberg.

16 *Princes et Grands dignitaires. Belzébuth, chef suprême ; Satan, prince détrôné ; Eurynome, prince de la Mort ; Moloch, prince du pays des Larmes ; Pluton, prince du Feu ; Pan, prince des Incubes ; Lilith, prince des Succubes ; Léonard,*

Berbiguier de Terre-Neuve du Thym struggled his whole life with mental illness, or with imps and demons, depending on whom you believe — him or his psychiatrist. Nevertheless, there is Lilith making a showing.

At the same time on the other side of the Channel, in 1820, the young Romantic poet John Keats brought Lilith as temptress to the attention of English-speaking readers with his long poem Lamia, a name that is the Latin translation of Lilith. She is a beautiful snake at first.

"She seem'd, at once, some penanced lady elf,
Some demon's mistress, or the demon's self.
Upon her crest she wore a wannish fire
Sprinkled with stars, like Ariadne's tiar:
Her head was serpent, but ah, bitter-sweet!
She had a woman's mouth with all its pearls complete:"[17]

---

grand-maître des sabbats ; Baalberith, grand pontife ; Proserpine, archi-diablesse. Berbigiuer, M. *The Imps, All The Demons Are Not From The Other World. 1821* This extraordinary book, a record of his encounters with demons, is cited as an example of outsider art by some critics. Berbiguier was committed to an asylum for a while under the care of that pioneer of psychotherapy, Dr Philippe Pinel.

17 Keats, John. 'The Lamia'

" She was a gordian shape of dazzling hue,
Vermilion-spotted, golden, green, and blue;
Striped like a zebra, freckled like a pard,
Eyed like a peacock, and all crimson barr'd;
And full of silver moons, that, as she breathed,
Dissolv'd, or brighter shone, or interwreathed
Their lustres with the gloomier tapestries—

And thus began Lilith's residence in the Victorian imagination. Her role as child-killer dropped away and that of seducer, man-eater and dangerous woman began to grow.

The plots of several of the very first novels in the new genre of fantasy literature, born in the 19th century, centred on dangerous, Lilith-like women. Perhaps the most complete re-imagining of Lilith was by George MacDonald, one of the fathers of modern fantasy fiction. His novel *Lilith: A Romance* was publishing in 1895 and tells a peculiar, sinister story of life after death and a battle between Lilith and Adam and Eve.

Earlier, English author Rider Haggard's best-selling fantasy, *She: A History of Adventure*, published 1865, explored elements of the Lilith archetype — a fierce, independent woman who plays by her own rules is the eponymous She, the queen of a secret land in the heart of Africa.

Oscar Wilde's play *Salomé*, a retelling of the Bible story about the beheading of John the Baptist, also plays with elements of the Lilith archetype, as rejected lover. Some have argued that the Salome story is a metaphor for castration,[18] as is the other Biblical narrative about a woman beheading a man, Judith.

So rainbow-sided, touch'd with miseries,
She seem'd, at once, some penanced lady elf,
Some demon's mistress, or the demon's self.
Upon her crest she wore a wannish fire
Sprinkled with stars, like Ariadne's tiar:
Her head was serpent, but ah, bitter-sweet!
She had a woman's mouth with all its pearls complete:
And for her eyes: what could such eyes do there
But weep, and weep, that they were born so fair?
As Proserpine still weeps for her Sicilian air.
Her throat was serpent, but the words she spake
Came, as through bubbling honey, for Love's sake,
And thus; while Hermes on his pinions lay,
Like a stoop'd falcon ere he takes his prey."

18 Neumann, Erich; tr. Ralph Manheim (1955). *The Great Mother.* Princeton: Princeton University Press. p. 168.

Lilith Envisioned

Artists had long been fascinated by the story of Judith, but in the Renaissance, beginning possibly with Lucas Cranach's depiction of a fashionably attired German vamp as Judith,[19] the subject of Judith beheading Holofernes changed in character from the depiction of a chaste national heroine of the Jewish people to that of a 'seducer-assassin'. This sexualised Judith is part of the Lilith archetype. The highly eroticised depictions of Judith painted in 1901 and 1909 by the Austrian artist, Gustav Klimt are part of this tradition and a reflection of the *fin de siècle* fascination with *femmes fatales*.

So far, the cultural sources cited have all been produced by men, obviously. But there is an outstanding example of a woman's interpretation of Judith: Artemisia Gentileschi's gory, visceral painting of Judith sawing off the head of Holofernes, painted 1612-13, is both startling and dramatic.[20] It also depicts an important element of the Lilith archetype: revenge.

In the mid-Victorian era, Lilith too was transformed from Middle Eastern demoness into a fashionable contemporary lady by Dante Gabriel Rossetti in his iconic painting *Lady Lilith*. Rossetti's Lilith has masses of strawberry blond hair, the whitest skin and beautiful bed clothes. She looks like an uncorsetted Victorian sex kitten. Rossetti's painting hints that beneath the exterior of an English rose, you might find a dangerous demoness. The wild is inside. This Lilith is very different from the wild haired women on the Jewish incantation bowls.

At the same time as the rediscovery or 'celebration' of dangerous women in European culture, in the West there was also a huge amount of interest in Indian religions, specifically the cult of Kali, a goddess also associated with severed heads, like Judith and Salome. She is often depicted wearing a belt of men's heads while she dances on the sleeping Shiva. The capital of British India until 1911 was Calcutta, which is still home to the most important Kali temple in the world at Kalighat. The earliest European ethnographers worked with the teachers at the Kali temple to translate

19 Jones, Jonathan. 'Judith with the Head of Holofernes.' *The Guardian*, 10 January 2004.

20 Sherwin, Skye. 'Artemisia Gentileschi's Judith Slaying Holofernes: A Vision of Vengeance.' *The Guardian*, 9 October 2020.

Vedic texts. From the beginning of the 19th century, these texts began to spread through scholarly circles across Europe, and by mid-century the idea of Kali, and her devoted, murderous followers, the thuggee, was part of popular imagination. Mind you, even the existence of such a cult is disputed now.

In other cultures, the Lilith archetype was never suppressed or cast out. For example, Kali worship has continued unbroken for centuries and probably millennia. It's not within the scope of this book to deal in depth with Kali, Durga, Minakshee and the other great goddesses of India, but simply to note that they represent similar ideas or energies to Lilith, and propose different ways of dealing with that energy too. After all, the Durga Puja in Bengal is still one of the biggest annual Indian festivals today. In Calcutta, hundreds of fabulous sculptures of the tiger-straddling, weapon-wielding goddess Durga are paraded through the streets and bathed in the water of the Hooghly every autumn and every community builds a *pandal*, a lodge where Durga lives for a few days.

Meanwhile back in Europe, as nature itself was receding during the rapid industrialisation of the 19th century, men and women were mourning — and discovering — the wildness in their own minds and souls. The new 'science' of psychotherapy was born at the end of the 19th century in the city and period that produced Klimt's vividly imagined Judith. With the hindsight of the 21st century, it's clear that much of the scaffolding of Sigmund Freud's theory of the human psyche seems to be based on male fears of women and of wildness.

Freud's younger contemporary, Carl Gustav Jung, took a more subtle approach, recognising that there is a creative power in the dark feminine. For him, the *anima* was the feminine side of a man's unconscious, while women had an *animus*, a male side to their unconscious. This description of the dark feminine side sometimes sounds a lot like Lilith. Following his lead, Jungians have written compellingly about the Lilith archetype, notably Sigmund Hurwitz, whose research into early Lilith is invaluable. Among many interesting observations, Hurwitz points out possible connections between Lilith and the Black Madonnas of Europe.[21]

The First World War did not dim the power of Lilith. Indeed, two early Nobel Prize winners of that time wrote about her. Lilith makes

21 Hurwitz, etc

an appearance in the form of the alluring Claudia Chauchat in Thomas Mann's masterpiece *The Magic Mountain*, set just before the war. It is the story of a young man in a TB clinic in the Alps, who is hopelessly in love with Madame Chauchat. Both are there, along with all the other inmates, because they are dying. The magic mountain itself is a place apart from the rest of the world, between this life and the next. Claudia is explicitly compared to Lilith by one of the philosophers with whom the hero Hans Castorp chats, recalling Goethe's description of her.[22]

> "Madame Chauchat had also adorned herself with a carnival cap – it wasn't even a bought one, but of the kind that children make, simply folded out of white paper into a three-cornered hat. She wore it crosswise and it suited her splendidly. The dark gold-brown silk dress swung above her feet; the skirt was a little loose. We will say nothing more about her arms here. They were naked up to the shoulder.
>
> "Take a close look at her!" Hans Castorp heard Signor Settembrini say as if from far away, while he followed her with his eyes, as she soon walked on, through the glass door and into the hall. "That is Lilith."
>
> "Who?" asked Hans Castorp.
>
> The writer was delighted by his question. He replied: "Adam's first wife. Watch out ..."
>
> Aside from the two of them, only Dr. Blumenkohl was still at the dinner table. The rest of the party, including Joachim, had moved to the drawing rooms. Hans Castorp said: "You are full of poetry and verse today. What kind of Lilli is that again? So was Adam married twice? I had no idea ...»
>
> "The Hebrew legend says so. This Lilith has become a night demon, dangerous for young men, especially because of her beautiful hair."

Across the channel, the British playwright George Bernard Shaw had a completely different take on the legend of Lilith. In his curious science-fiction masterwork, *Back to Methuselah: A Metabiological Pentateuch*, premiered on 27 February 1922, Lilith is re-imagined as the mother of

22 From *The Magic Mountain* page 549

both Adam and Eve and therefore all humanity. Shaw gives Lilith the last word, some time far in the future, around 30,000 AD when humans live for a very long time:

> "I am Lilith: I brought life into the whirlpool of force, and compelled my enemy, Matter, to obey a living soul. But in enslaving Life's enemy I made him Life's master; for that is the end of all slavery; and now I shall see the slave set free and the enemy reconciled, the whirlpool become all life and no matter."

At the time, Shaw was probably the most famous writer in the English language, so even his less popular works, such as this one, influenced public discourse, and Mann was the most famous writer in German, so ditto. Lilith was evolving.

The Pagan Revival

The return of Lilith to public consciousness in the late 19th and 20th century was part of the wider revival of paganism. As the rural world of Europe faded, attempts began to remember, preserve and even restore the patterns and rural ways that were fast disappearing. Folklorists, composers and collectors of tales, like the Brothers Grimm, collected stories and songs, recorded dances and patterns of speech. At the same time, in England and across the channel in France, new occultists among the educated classes sought to find roots in the soil and in history. *The Zohar*, with its various references to Lilith, was a source used by one of the new occult's most influential writers, Eliphas Levi. In the mid-19th century, Levi wrote 20 books on the occult which were widely read.

At the same as this creative rediscovery of western mysticism was taking place, so was a revival of interest in the witch trials of previous centuries and a reframing of those too. The highly influential French popular historian Jules Michelet published *La Sorcière*, a study of the history of witchcraft in 1862. He proposed that witches were real, rebels against the oppressions of the feudal world, and they were the remnants of a pagan religion that had thrived in Europe right into the middle ages.[23]

Both these strands, which included different traces of Lilith, twined together to weave the modern neo-pagan movement, and unsurprisingly

23 Hutton, Ronald. *The Triumph of the Moon: A History of Modern Pagan Witchcraft*

Lilith, the first witch, is a central figure for many modern practitioners of the craft. Google Lilith today and you will be led to any number of websites and forums where readers discuss the arcana of worshipping their particular version of this ancient power-figure: bride of Satan or feminist role-model, independent woman or leader of a coven?

Astrology

Naturally, the interest in Lilith at the end of the 19th century did not pass by astrologers, who were closely involved with the Belle Époque revival of magic and paganism.

The first mention of an astrological Lilith was in connection with a hypothetical second Moon posited by the astronomer Georg Walthemath. At the dawn of the 20th century the well-known British astrologer Sepharial named this point Lilith, because "she was the dark moon of the same nature as Delilah, betrayer of men".[24] Unfortunately, there is no such body, although some astrologers refer to this point still.

In 1927, a real physical asteroid was named Lilith, after the much-mourned pianist Lili Boulanger, who had died tragically young in 1918. The asteroid was discovered by the astronomer Benjamin Jekhowsky, a fellow White Russian, on 11 February. I checked Lili Boulanger's natal chart to see the position of this asteroid, and found that in fact, the point that was rising when Boulanger was born was actually another astrological Lilith, our Lilith, the Black Moon, which would be named in the following decade.

Astrologers were intent on finding a more powerful place for Adam's first wife in the panoply of the sky. The next point to be named after Lilith was the apogee of the Moon, that is the point furthest from Earth on the Moon's orbit. Dom Néroman, a prolific author and founder of the *Collège Astrologique de France*, is often given credit for the introduction of Black Moon Lilith to the astrological canon in 1937. But his source for this remains obscure — and perhaps that is an interesting part of the Lilith story. All the sources are obscure — from the origin of her story in

24 Farnell, Kim. *The Astral Tramp: A Biography of Sepharial*. I spoke with Farnell, the world expert on Sepharial, about this subject and she believes that in all likelihood Sepharial was pondering Lilith as early as 1898, about 20 years before it is generally supposed.

Sumeria, to her appearance in *The Alphabet of Ben Sirah,* to her arrival in the astrological software of the 21st century.

What is certain is that unlike, say, Pluto or Neptune, there is no specific date for the discovery of the astrological Lilith. But the naming of this point does emerge from that tumultuous period in Europe between the wars — a time when the ideas of Freud lit artistic and intellectual circles, fascism and nationalism were on the rise, women were beginning to reclaim political and economic power, and economies crashed and burned.

Néroman himself, whose real name was Pierre Maurice Rougié, survived the war in fighting spirit, mainly arguing with other astrologers, and died in the early 1950s. Many of his ideas now seem surprising — for example, he assigned Uranus to Pisces — but Black Moon Lilith had arrived in the astrological canon and she is here to stay. Since Néroman, most of the serious work on the astrological Lilith has taken place in mainland Europe. This book is an attempt to bring our understanding of the astrological Lilith up-to-date, and to make her as important a point in interpretation as, say, the Nodes of the Moon.

Feminism

In the 1970s, second wave feminism fell in love with Lilith, this time as a symbol of autonomy and sexual freedom, the first feminist who rebelled against patriarchal authority. The seed for this may have been a 1972 essay by Judith Plaskow, an American feminist theologian and Hebrew scholar, entitled *The Coming of Lilith* in which she re-imagines the story of Adam's first wife. In Plaskow's version of the myth, Lilith and Eve co-operate. This was, consciously or not, an echo of Robert Browning's late Victorian poem about Lilith and Eve.

In the 20th century, Jewish feminists in particular found in Lilith an ancient role model for freedom from the patriarchy, naming the Jewish feminist magazine *Lilith*, first published in 1976 and still going strong. Using the story of Lilith as a jumping off point, Plaskow argued that Judaism is actually a religion of equality not patriarchy. Since then, the Hebrew Lilith has become a widely accepted feminist symbol of independence.

At the confluence of feminism and neopaganism is modern Wicca. Lilith has been raised to the status of goddess by some adherents of the craft. Some seem to worship her truly dark side, the baby-killer, taboo breaker, satanic wife, drinker of blood, others focus on the erotic, the magical, the wild and free-spirited independent goddess.

Popular Culture

In the arts, simmering interest in Lilith since the 19th century, bursts regularly into a boil. She is always reshaped to fit the times. For example, in the 1960s, *Lilith* was the beautiful mad girl in the eponymous movie starring Jean Seberg. Octavia Butler's classic feminist sci-fi novel, *Lilith's Brood*, published in the 1980s, is about a post-apocalyptic world, in which humans must mate with aliens to survive, creating a new kind of being, an interesting reinvention of the Hebrew legend of Lilith breeding hundreds of babies with her lover in the desert wastes.

Like all the great archetypes in late stage capitalism, Lilith has been commodified, repackaged for television, *anime* and video games. In fact, in the second decade of the 21st century, she popped up so regularly in games and cartoons that many viewers and players must have become quite familiar with her as a demoness and seducer, for this is how she was usually portrayed. The name Lilith became a shorthand for sexy bad girl, with possible demonic tendencies. On TV, Lilith so far has been more of a second tier character. In the long-running 90s sit-com *Frasier*, Lilith was the name of the eponymous hero's first, terrifying wife, played by Bebe Neuwirth, who has appropriately a *Via Lamia* that runs right across her Descendant. Since then, Lilith has appeared in all kinds of shows from *Scooby-Doo* to *Lucifer*. However, even when she is not named as Lilith we recognise her in independent, powerful heroines from Samantha in *Sex and the City* to Jean Milburn in *Sex Education*. In 2024, a character called Lilith was played by Cate Blanchett in the truly awful *Borderlands*, the movie version of the video game.

So like all great archetypes, Lilith is born and reborn again, made new for every generation, but also made new within each of us. She may be jostling for position among all the characters we each contain.

For a long time, she was suppressed and cast out. She was not invited to the table, but now it's time to ask her in, treat her politely and maybe apologise for all those years of desert-dwelling. Welcome her back into your own Edenic place, and see what you can work out together.

Astrological Charts

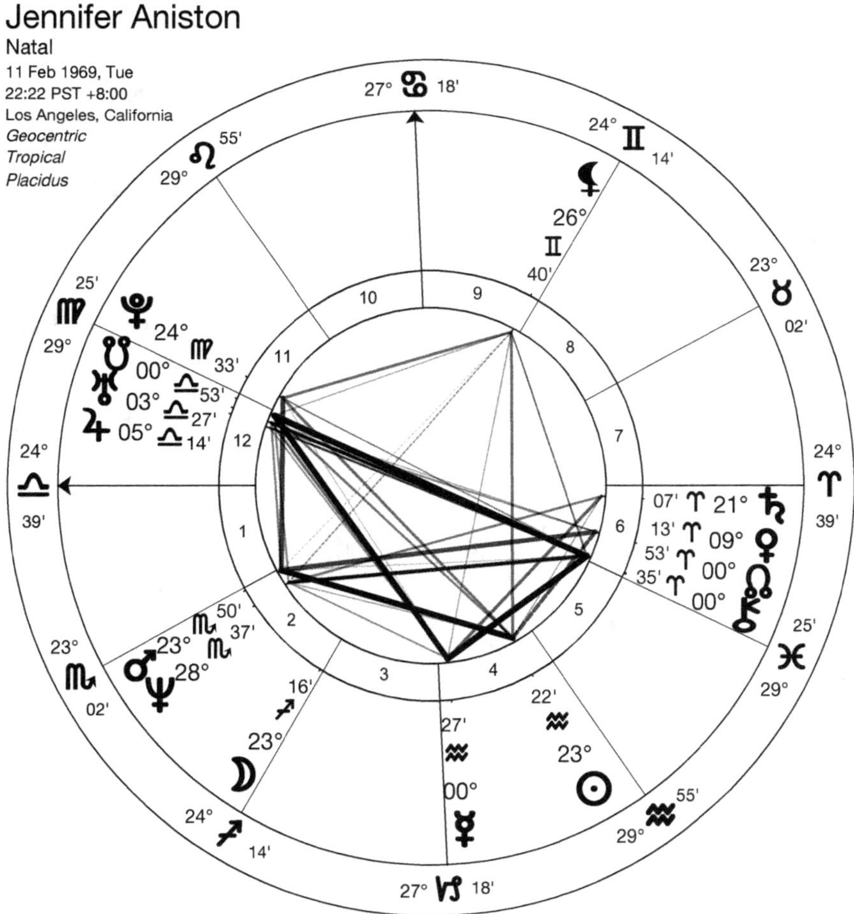

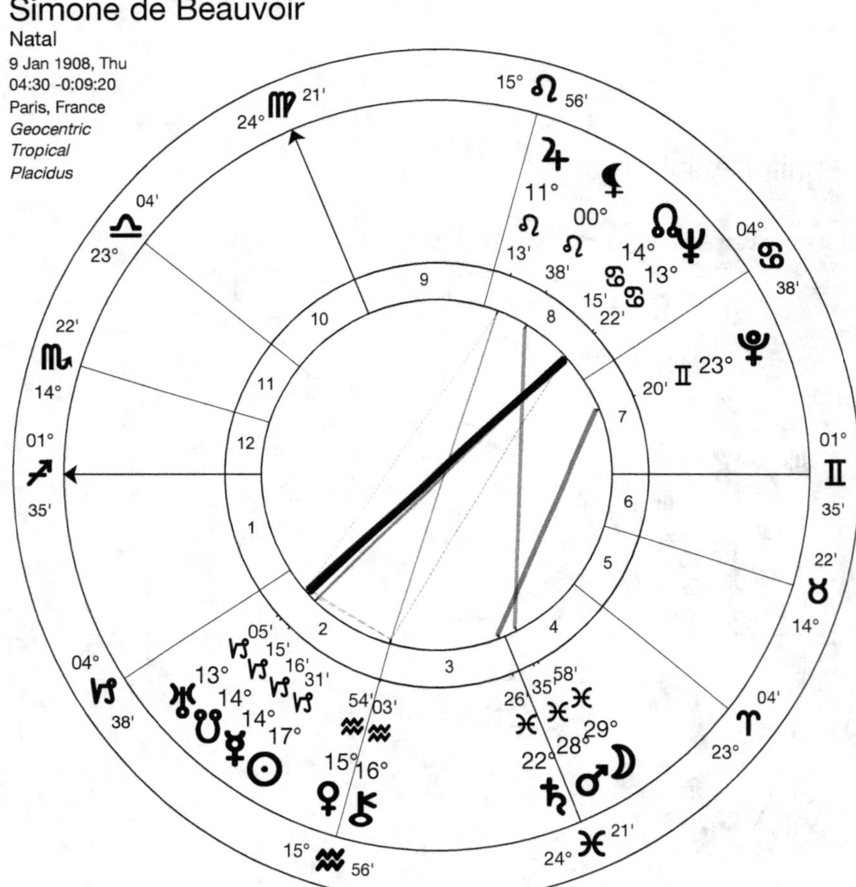
Simone de Beauvoir
Natal
9 Jan 1908, Thu
04:30 -0:09:20
Paris, France
Geocentric
Tropical
Placidus

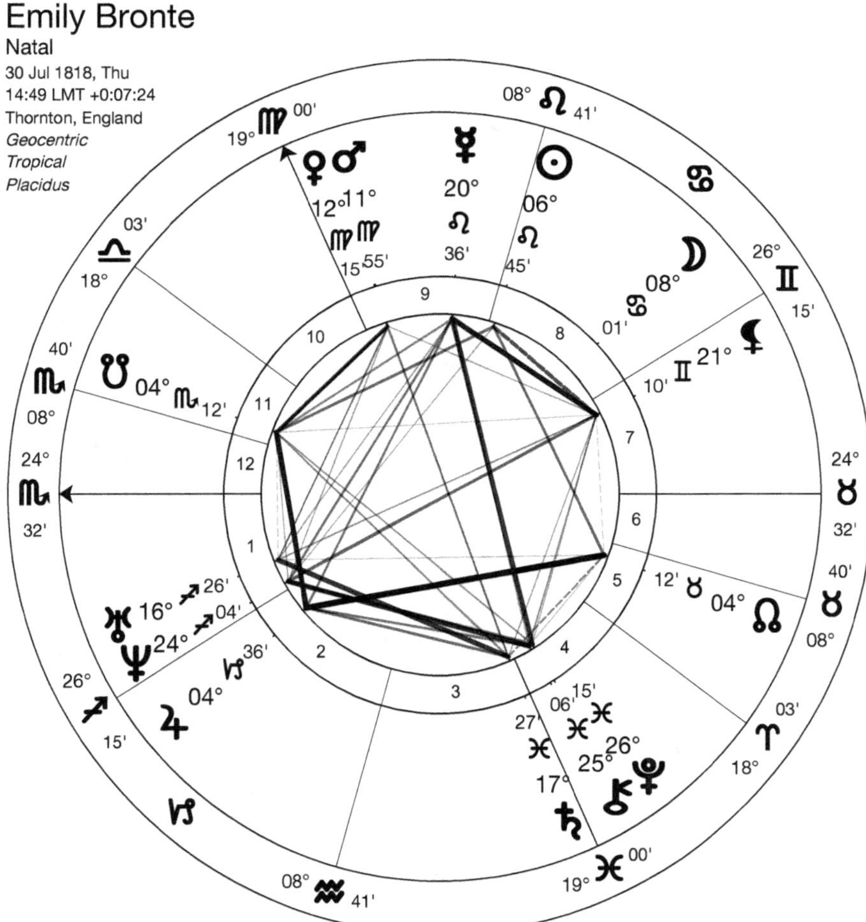
Emily Bronte
Natal
30 Jul 1818, Thu
14:49 LMT +0:07:24
Thornton, England
Geocentric
Tropical
Placidus

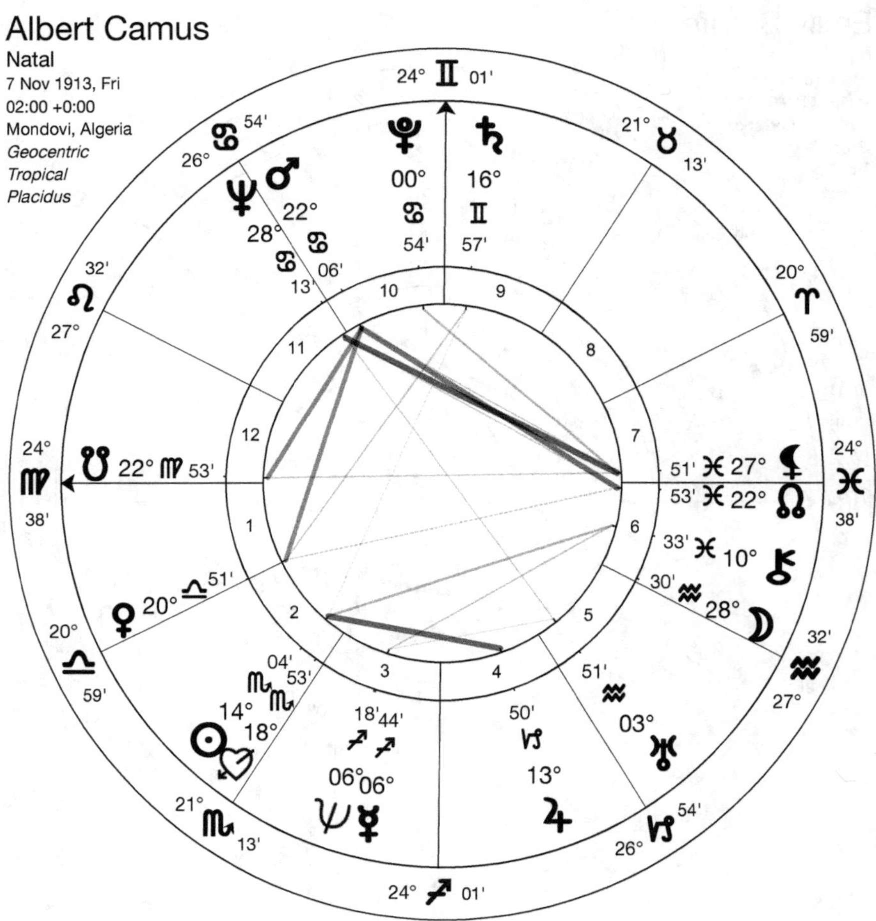
Albert Camus
Natal
7 Nov 1913, Fri
02:00 +0:00
Mondovi, Algeria
Geocentric
Tropical
Placidus

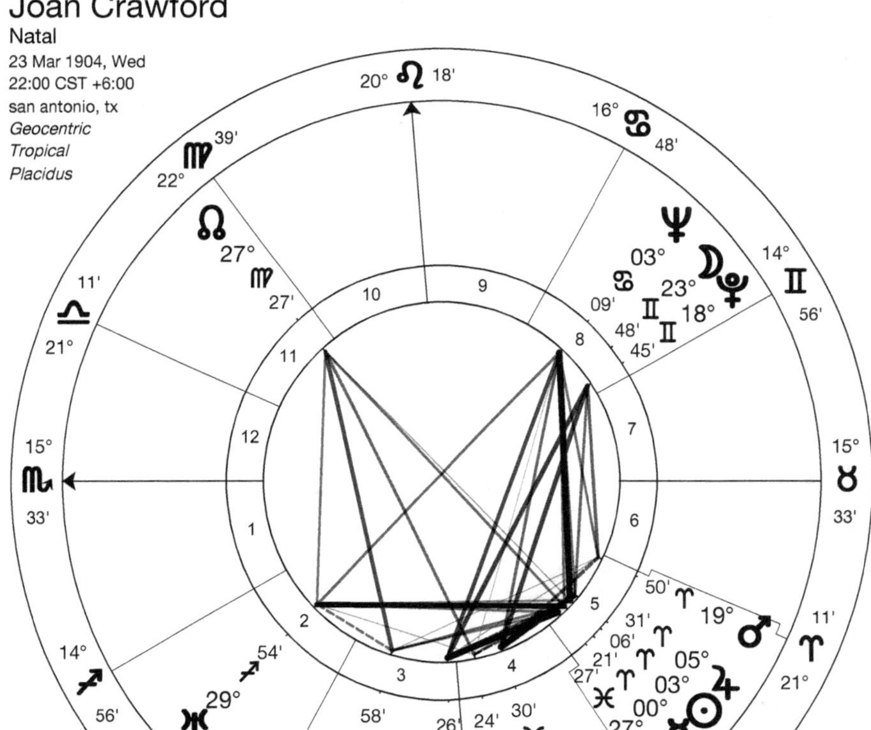
Joan Crawford
Natal
23 Mar 1904, Wed
22:00 CST +6:00
san antonio, tx
Geocentric
Tropical
Placidus

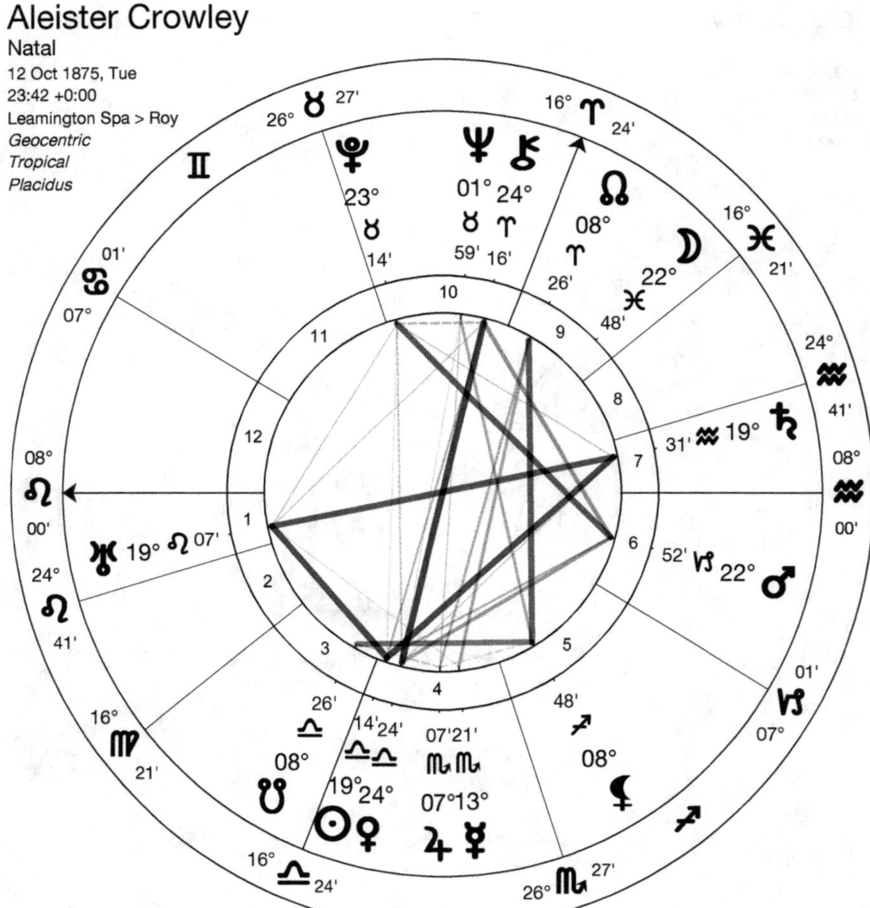
Aleister Crowley
Natal
12 Oct 1875, Tue
23:42 +0:00
Leamington Spa > Roy
Geocentric
Tropical
Placidus

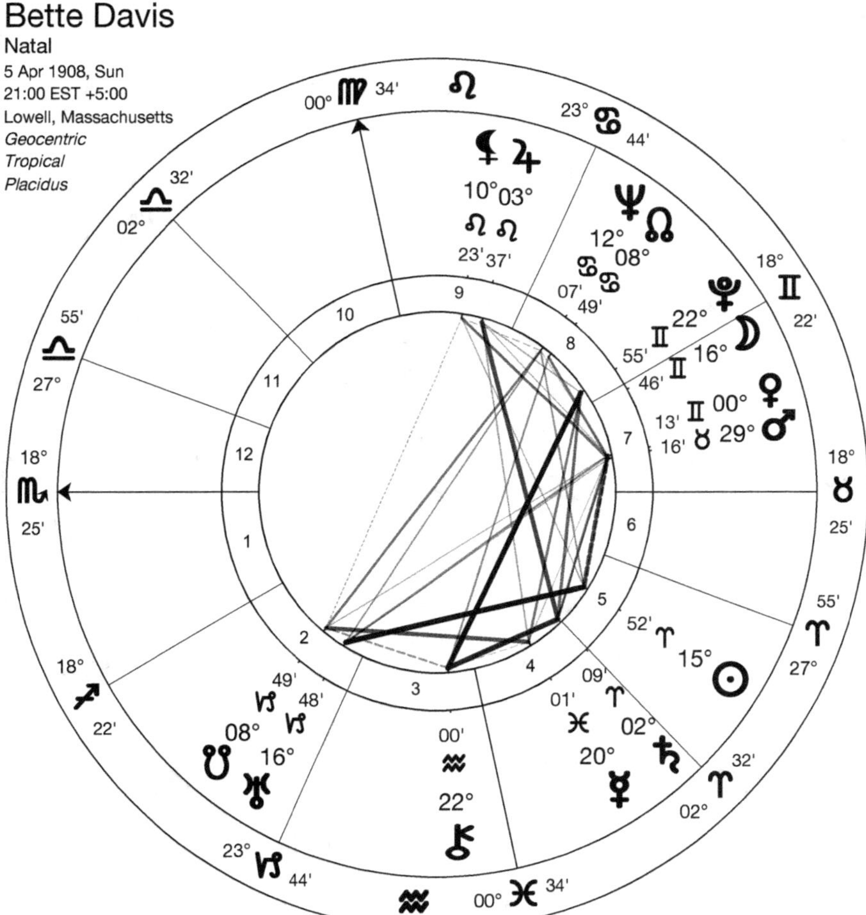
Bette Davis
Natal
5 Apr 1908, Sun
21:00 EST +5:00
Lowell, Massachusetts
Geocentric
Tropical
Placidus

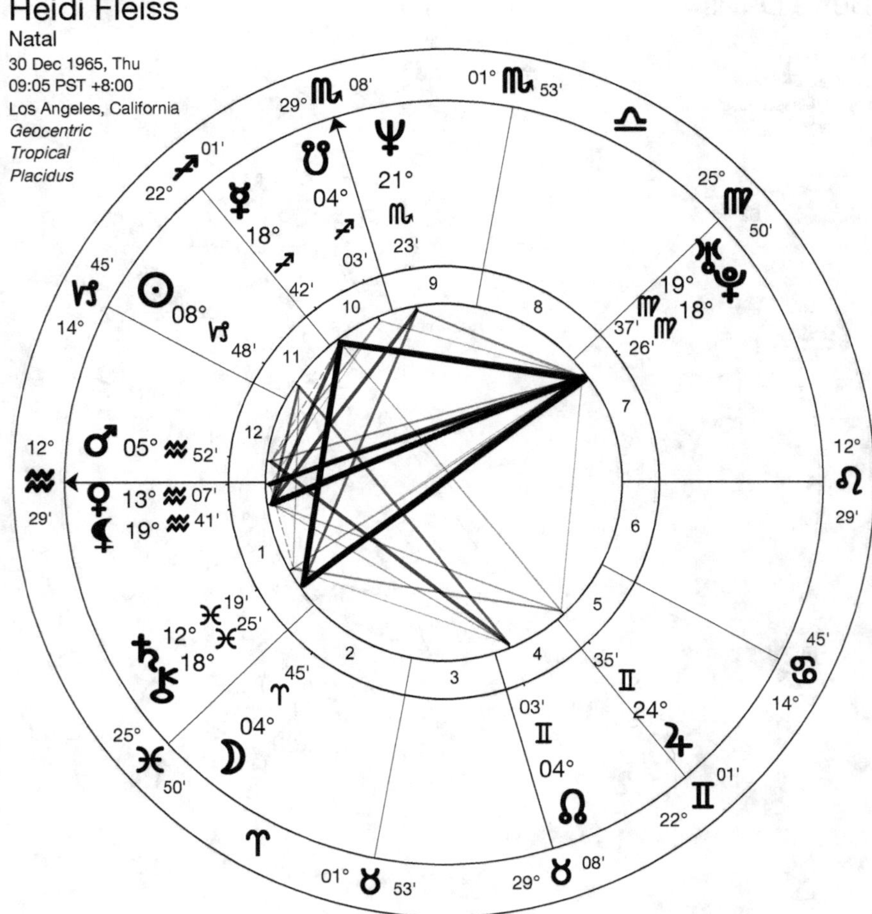
Heidi Fleiss
Natal
30 Dec 1965, Thu
09:05 PST +8:00
Los Angeles, California
Geocentric
Tropical
Placidus

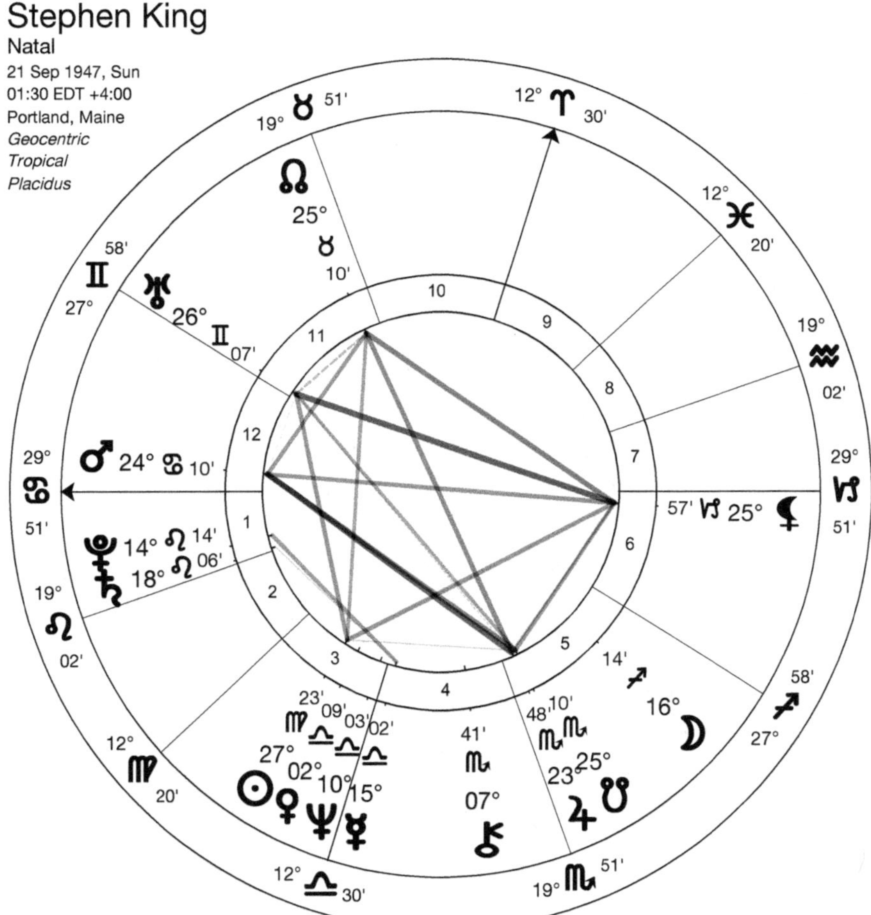
Stephen King
Natal
21 Sep 1947, Sun
01:30 EDT +4:00
Portland, Maine
Geocentric
Tropical
Placidus

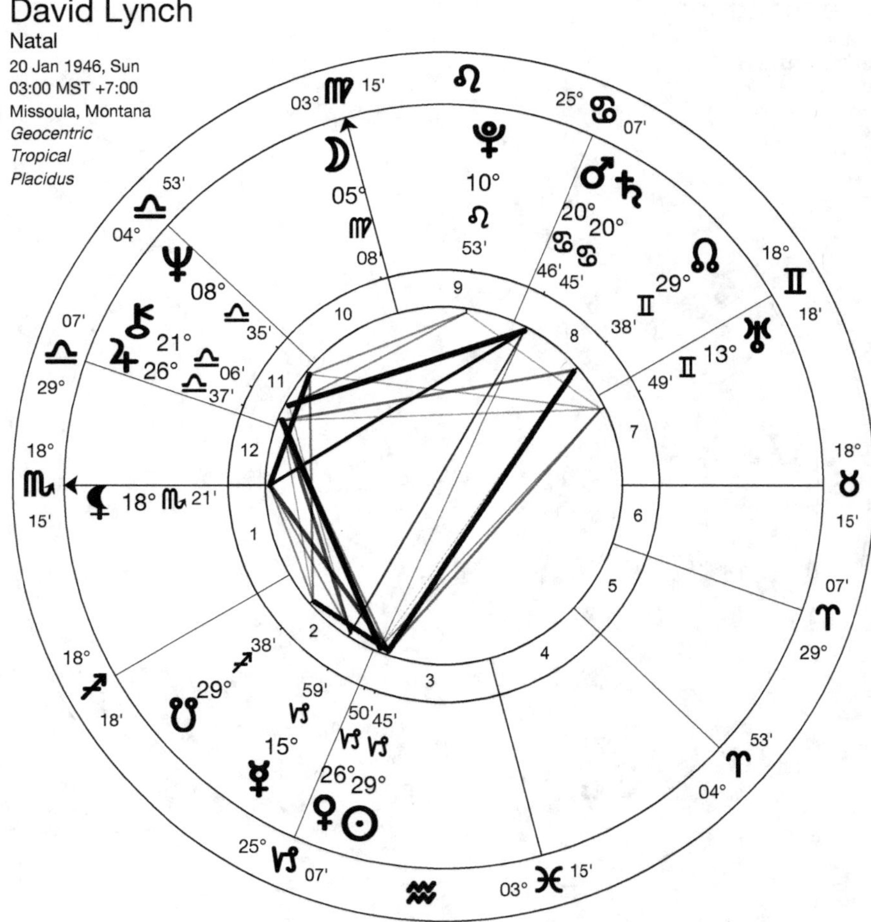
David Lynch
Natal
20 Jan 1946, Sun
03:00 MST +7:00
Missoula, Montana
Geocentric
Tropical
Placidus

Gustav Mahler

Natal

7 Jul 1860, Sat

22:19 -0:57:44

Praha, Czech Republic

Geocentric

Tropical

Placidus

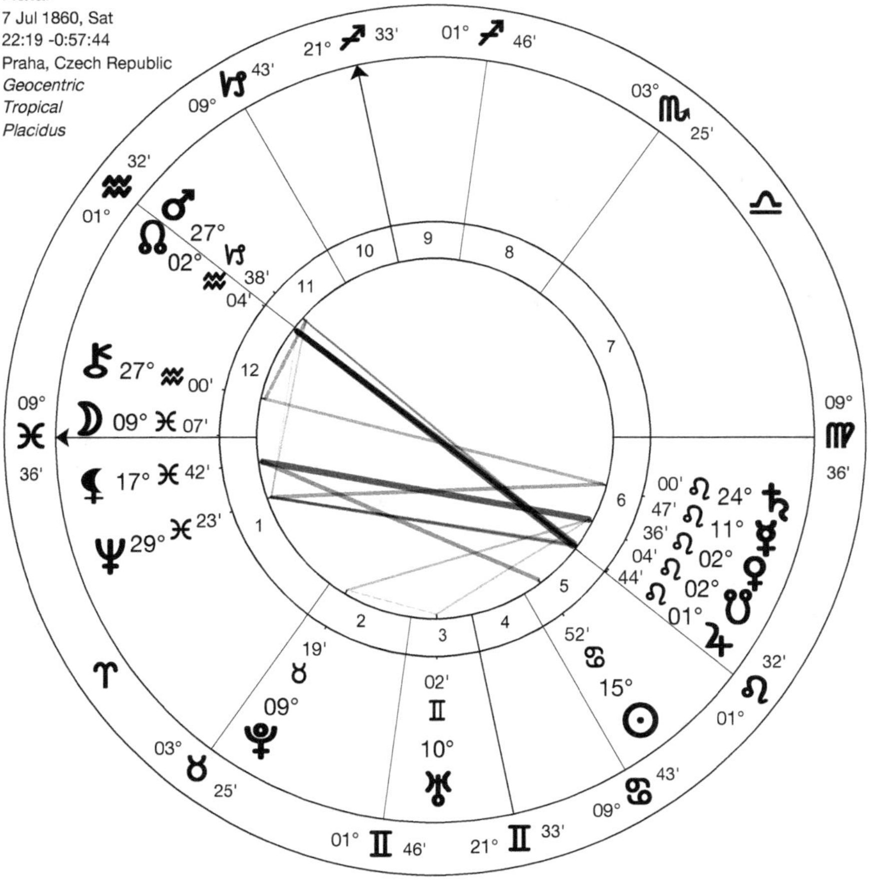

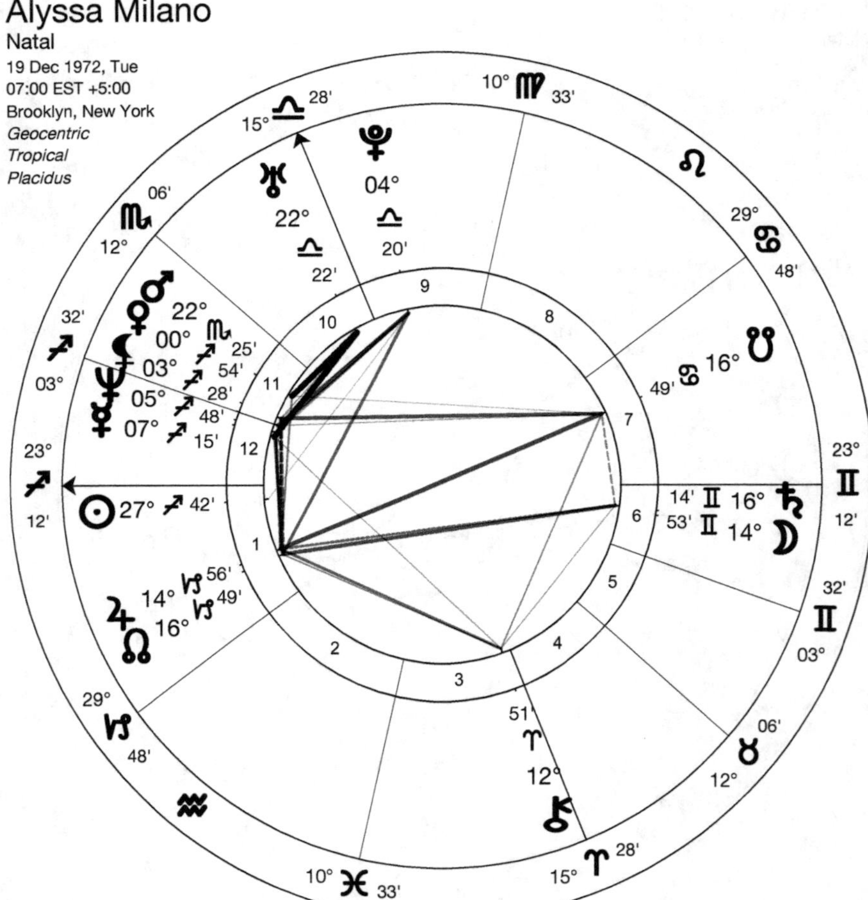
Alyssa Milano
Natal
19 Dec 1972, Tue
07:00 EST +5:00
Brooklyn, New York
Geocentric
Tropical
Placidus

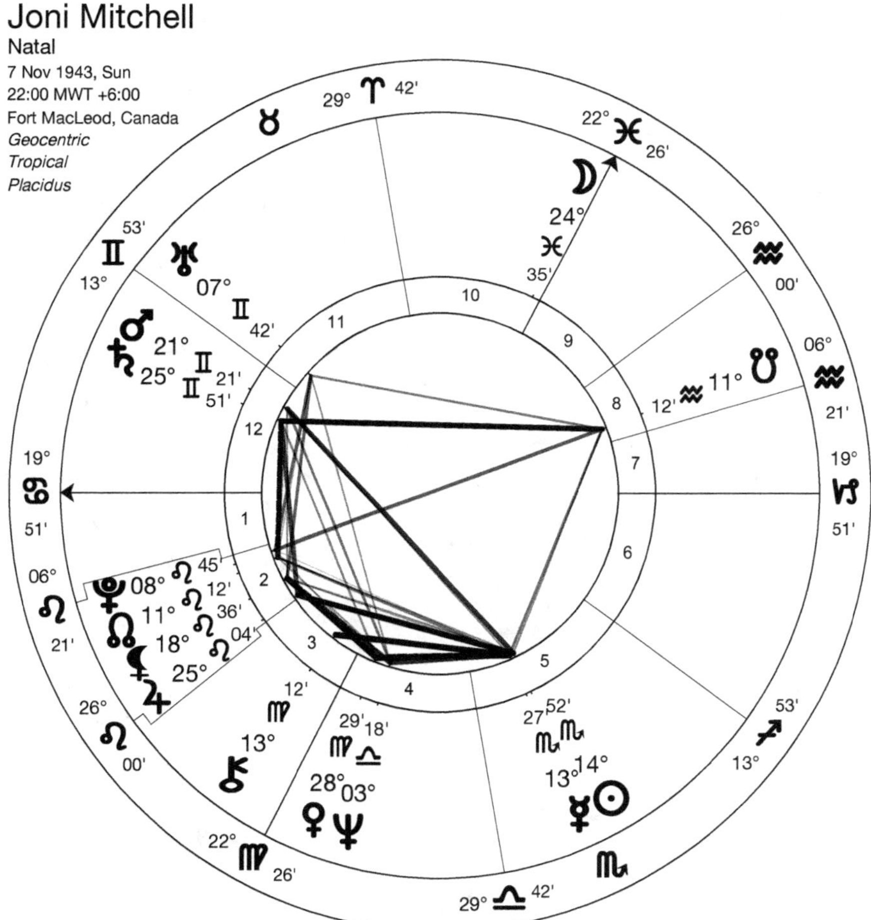
Joni Mitchell
Natal
7 Nov 1943, Sun
22:00 MWT +6:00
Fort MacLeod, Canada
Geocentric
Tropical
Placidus

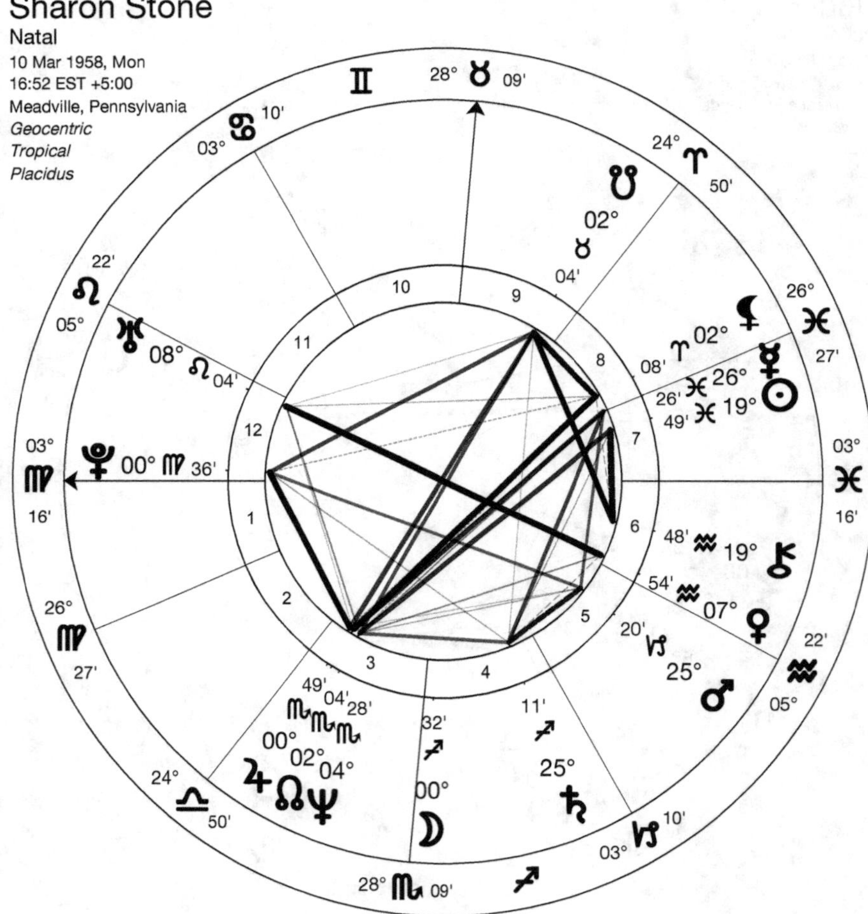
Sharon Stone
Natal
10 Mar 1958, Mon
16:52 EST +5:00
Meadville, Pennsylvania
Geocentric
Tropical
Placidus

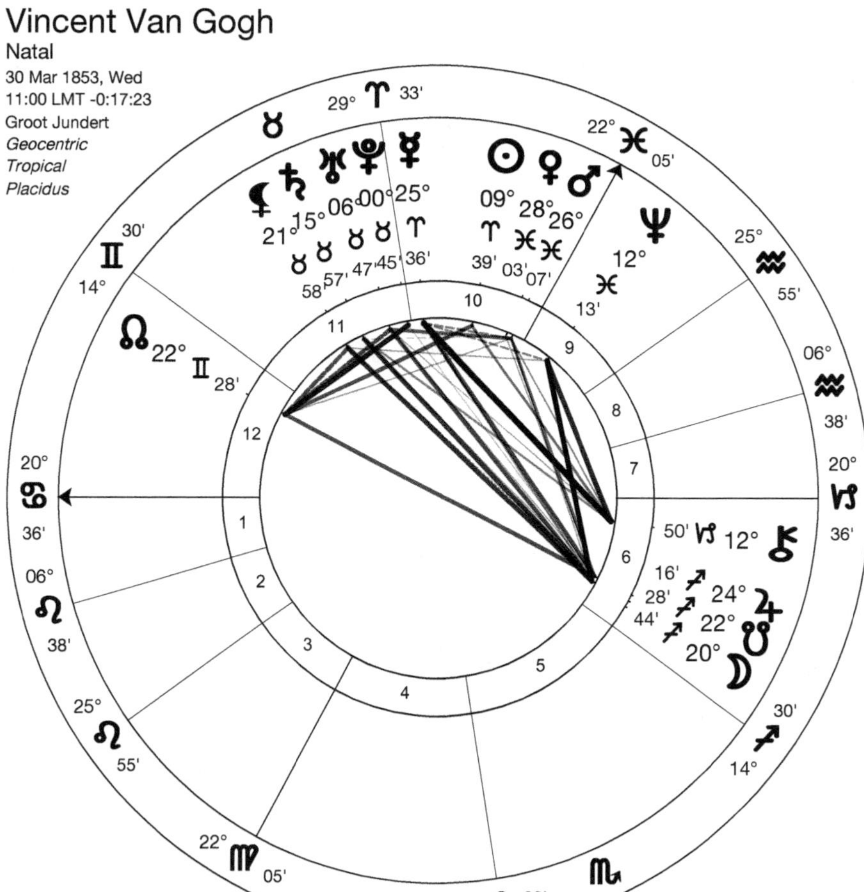
Vincent Van Gogh
Natal
30 Mar 1853, Wed
11:00 LMT -0:17:23
Groot Jundert
Geocentric
Tropical
Placidus

Phoebe Waller-Bridge (time unknown)

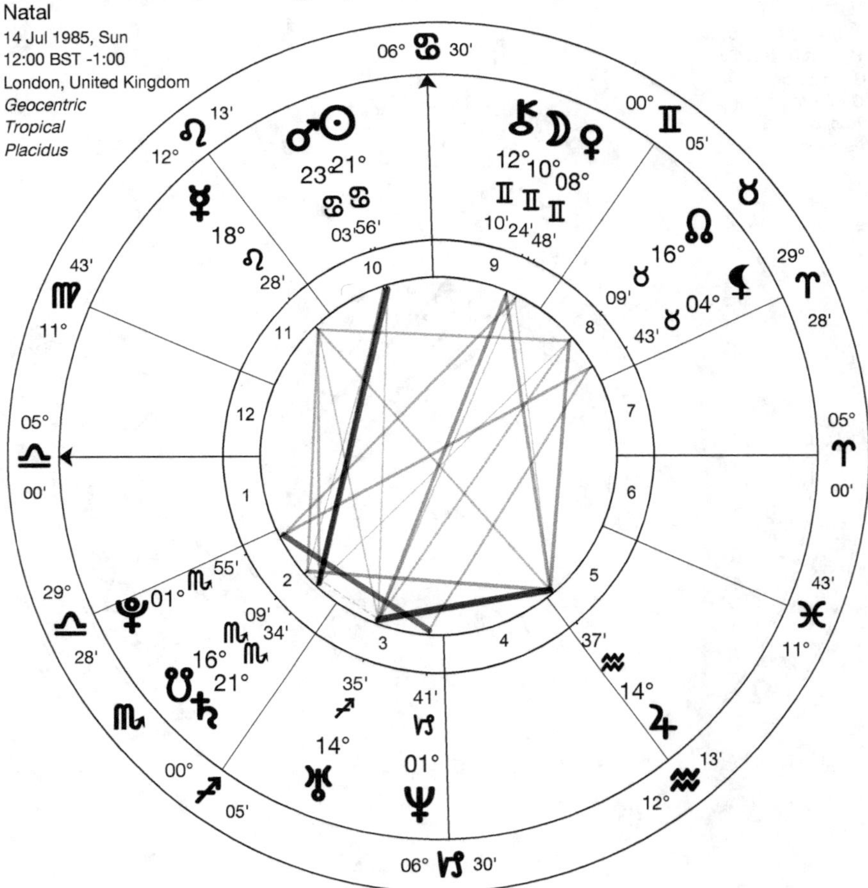

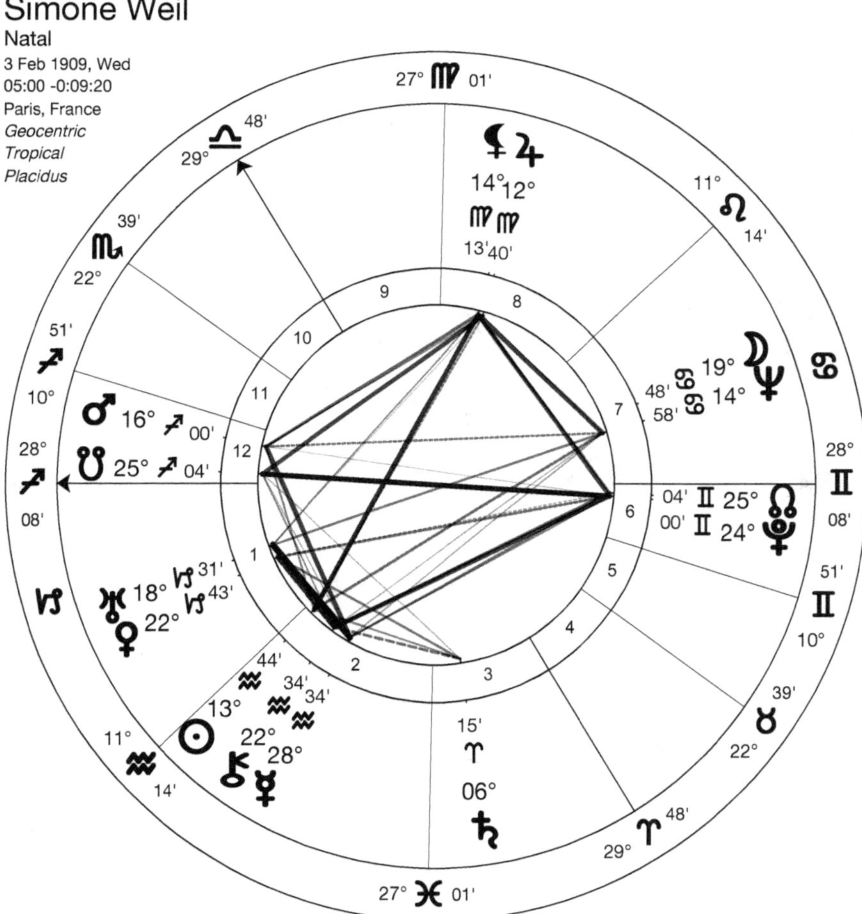
Simone Weil
Natal
3 Feb 1909, Wed
05:00 -0:09:20
Paris, France
Geocentric
Tropical
Placidus

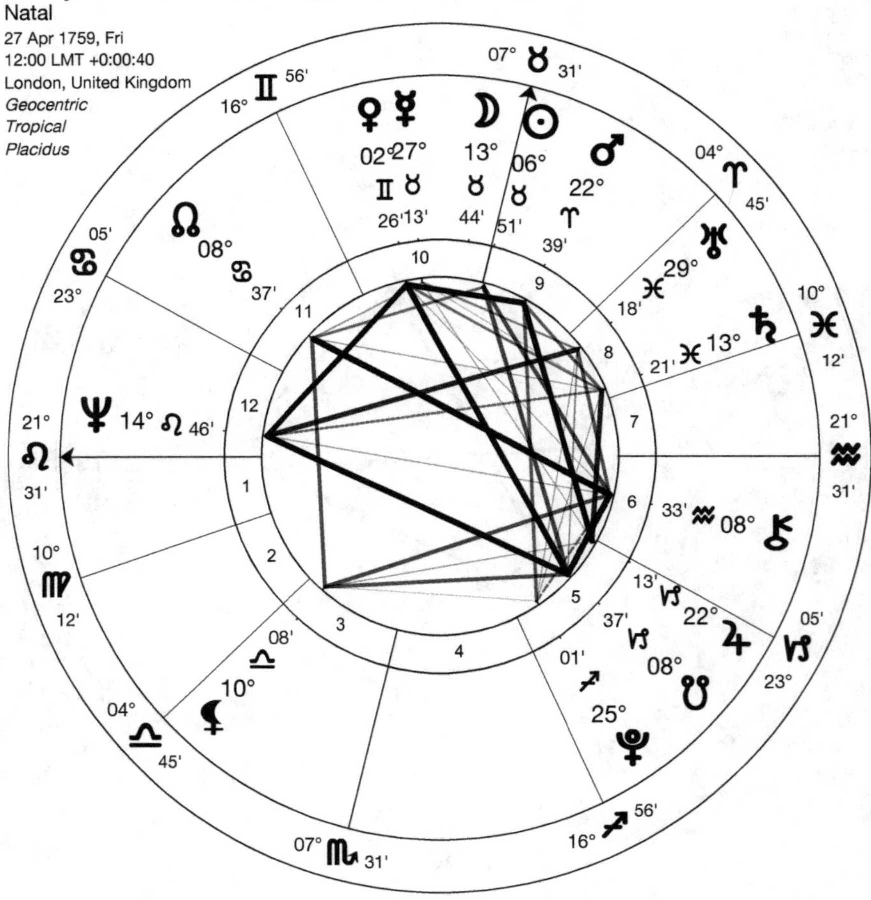
Mary Wollstonecraft (time unknown)
Natal
27 Apr 1759, Fri
12:00 LMT +0:00:40
London, United Kingdom
Geocentric
Tropical
Placidus

Picture Credits

Part openers

p.1 HJ Ford 'The Shepherd Comes to the Arch of Snakes' from *The Crimson Fairy Book*

p.23 HJ Ford 'The Enchanted Snake' from *The Green Fairy Book*

p.127 HJ Ford 'Soothing the Serpent King' from *The Violet Fairy Book*

p.135 Albrecht Dürer. *Adam and Eve.*

Signs of the Zodiac

Aries

Henri Matisse, Self Portrait, 1937, charcoal with stumping on laid paper.

National Gallery of Art, Washington DC. Collection of Mr and Mrs Paul Mellon.

Taurus

Dora Wahlroos, Self-Portrait, 1901, oil on panel, Finnish National Gallery

Collection/Ateneum Art Museum Photo: Finnish National Gallery/ Hannu Aaltonen

Gemini

Henri Fantin-Latour, Self Portrait, 1860, chalk and charcoal on paper. © Musee d'Orsay, Dist. RMN-Grand Palais/Patrice Schmidt

Cancer

Frida Kahlo, Self Portrait with Thorn Necklace and Hummingbird, 1940, oil on canvas on masonite. The Nickolas Muray Collection of Mexican Art at the Harry Ransom Center at the University of Texas at Austin.

Leo

Egon Schiele, Self Portrait (unfinished), 1912, watercolour on paper. Private Collection.

Virgo

Henry Fuseli, Self Portrait, c.1777, chalk on paper. © National Portrait Gallery, London.

Libra

Shima Seien, *Mudai* [*Untitled*], 1918, 85 × 108 cm, Osaka City Museum of Fine Arts, © Osaka City Museum of Fine Arts

Scorpio

Clara von Rappard, Selbstbildnis, 1890, Ol auf Leinwand, 97 x 76,7 cm, Kunstmuseum Bern, Image credits: Kunstmuseum Bern

Sagittarius

Zinaida Serebriakova, At the Dressing-Table (Self Portrait), 1909, oil on canvas, Tretyakov Gallery, Moscow, Russia.

Capricorn

Kathe Kollwitz (1867-1945), Self Portrait, 1924, Crayon Lithograph, Kn 209 b, Kathe Kollwitz Collection in Cologne

Aquarius

Jo Koster, Self-Portrait with Eyepatch, 1939, oil on canvas. Private collection.

Pisces

Albrecht Durer, Self Portrait, Study of Hand and Pillow, 1493. Metropolitan Museum of Art, New York, New York.

Houses and Angles

p.97 Ella Fitzgerald image courtesy the Fraser MacPherson estate c/o Guy MacPherson, licensed under the Creative Commons Attribution 2.0 Generic license: https://creativecommons.org/licenses/by/2.0/

Background

p.141 *Lamia, La Belle Dame sans Merci*, &c by John Keats. Early 20th century edition published by George Routledge & Sons Ltd in London and E.P. Dutton & Co. in New York. Cover illustration by R. Gardner.

p.142 The Climax, plate X for Oscar Wilde's *Salome.* Line block print of an illustration by Aubrey Beardsley, drawn 1893. Printed in Germany, 1907.

Further Reading

Non-fiction

add Begg, Ean, *The Cult of the Black Virgin*, Deep Books (2007)

Bigé, Luc. *La Lune Noire: Un Vertige Absolu.* Janus 2019

Black Koltuv, Barbara. *The Book of Lilith.* Hays Ltd. (1986)

Gimbutas, Marija. *The Living Goddesses.* University of California Press (2001)

Hunter, Kelley. *Living Lilith: Four Dimensions of the Cosmic Feminine.* Wessex Astrologer (2009)

Hurwitz, Sigmund. *The First Eve: Historical and Psychological Aspects of the Dark Feminine.* Daimon (2012)

McDonald, Beth E., *In Possession of the Night: Lilith as Goddess, Demon, Vampire* (2009). Sabbath, Roberta Sternman (ed)

Rivlin, Lilly. 'Lilith'. *Ms Magazine* (1972)

Fiction and Poetry

Baudelaire, Charles. *The Flowers of Evil.* OUP (2008)

Bronte, Emily. *Wuthering Heights.* Thomas Cautley Newby et al. (First published 1847)

Burton, Jesse. *Medusa.* Bloomsbury (2023)

Butler, Octavia E. *Lilith's Brood.* Grand Central Publishing Ltd (1987-1989)

Camus, Albert. *The Stranger.* Gallimard et al (first published in French 1942)

Dove, Rita. *Mother Love.* W. W. Norton (1995)

Ferrante, Elena. *The Neapolitan Quartet.* Europa Publishing (2012-2014)

Flaubert, Gustav. *Madame Bovary.* Michel Levy Freres et al. (First published 1857)

Hardy, Thomas. *Tess of the D'Urbervilles.* James R. Osgood, McIlvaine & Co et al. (First published 1891)

Highsmith, Patricia. *The Ripliad.* Alfred A. Knopf et al. (1955-1991)

Jackson, Shirley. *We Have Always Lived in the Castle.* Viking (1962)

MacDonald, George. *Lilith.* Chatto and Windus. First published 1895

Mistral, Gabriela. *Selected Poems* translated by Ursula Le Guin. University of New Mexico Press (2011)

Morrison, Toni. *Beloved.* Alfred A. Knopf (1987)

O'Brien, Edna. *The Country Girls Trilogy.* Faber & Faber (2019)

Oliver, Mary. *Devotions* (2017)

Rendell, Ruth. (who also writes as Barbara Vine): The figure of Lilith is a recurring character in Rendell's work, notably, for example, in *The Bridesmaid.* When she writes as Barbara Vine, there is often a more sympathetic type of Lilith outsider or even narrator in several cases.

Rhys, Jean. *Wide Sargasso Sea.* André Deutsch (1966)

Rimbaud, Arthur. *Rimbaud Complete.* Modern Library Inc. (2003)

Rossetti, Christina. *Selected Poems: Rossetti.* Penguin. (2008)

Further Viewing

Lilith-style characters are a staple of story-telling, and you will find avatars of her, or him, in many films and TV shows. This is a short list to get you thinking and dreaming.

Aliens, dir James Cameron, 1986

All That Heaven Allows, dir Douglas Sirk, 1955

Bande A Part, Jean Luc Goddard, 1964

Betty Blue, dir Jean Jacques Beineix, 1986

Black Moon, dir Louis Malle, 1975

Breaking the Waves, dir Lars von Trier, 1996

Children of Men, dir Alfonso Cuaron, 2006

Cleo from 5 to 7, Agnes Varda, 1962

Crash, dir David Cronenberg, 1996

Die My Love, dir Lynne Ramsay, 2025

Empire of the Sun, dir Steven Spielberg, 1987

Far From Heaven, Todd Haynes, 2002

Heroic Trio, Johnnie To, 1993

Jeanne Dielman, 23 Quai du Commerce, Bruxelles, dir Chantal Akerman, 1975

Johnny Guitar, dir Nicholas Ray, 1954

Kiki's Delivery Service, dir Hayao Miyazaki, 1989

La Strada, dir Federico Fellini, 1954

Les Amants du Pont Neuf, dir Leos Carax, 1991

Lilith, dir Robert Rossen, 1964

Mildred Pierce — both the Joan Crawford film, dir Michael Curtis, 1945, and the Kate Winslet miniseries, dir Todd Haynes, 2011

Morvern Callar, dir Lynne Ramsay, 2002

My Brilliant Career, dir Gillian Armstrong, 1979

Rocky Horror Picture Show, dir Jim Sharman, 1975.

Single White Female, dir Barbet Schroeder, 1992

Taxi Driver, dir Martin Scorsese, 1976

The Age of Innocence, dir Martin Scorsese, 1993

The Deep Blue Sea, Terence Davies, 2011

The Hunger Games, dir Gary Ross, 2012

The Night of the Hunter, dir Charles Laughton, 1955

The Talented Mr Ripley, dir Anthony Minghella, 1999

The Substance, dir Coralie Fargeat, 2024

Twin Peaks (TV), 1990, and *Blue Velvet* (film), 1986, dir David Lynch

Unrelated, Joanna Hogg, 2007

Vagabonde, dir Agnes Varda, 1985

Woman in the Dunes, dir Hiroshi Teshigahara, 1964

Acknowledgments

Many thanks to Ciaran Cosgrove for his kind permission to reprint his translation of Gabriela Mistral's poem The Foreigner. It was first published in *Poetry Ireland Review* Issue 18/19.

Thanks also for kind permission to print a portion of Rita Dove's poem, *Persephone, Falling* from WW Norton.

Thanks to the estate of Frank O'Hara and City Lights Books for permission to reprint part of *Ave Maria.*

Index

N

O

T

www.ingramcontent.com/pod-product-compliance
Lightning Source LLC
LaVergne TN
LVHW020045110826
845155LV00029B/635

* 9 7 8 1 9 1 6 6 2 5 3 7 2 *